Praise for Rebel Housewife Rules

"At long last a dose of reality on the subject of marriage and family. Filled with many needed-to-be-heeded realistic tips on how to juggle it all. You'll find yourself laughing out loud at this survivors' guide to domestic life. My husband even swiped my copy and had a few knowing laughs of his own! These gals know the one thing you can't live without at home—a sense of humor!"

—Lisa Hammond, author of *Dream Big* and founder of Femail Creations

"You mean it's not all domestic bliss?! As a single gal still in search of her 'Prince Charming,' I first read Sherri and Vicki's hilarious book wondering if being single wasn't so bad after all!

"They dispelled every myth I ever had about life on the other side! But read between the lines— you'll also find two incredible, funny women who may have given up their 'dream careers,' but discovered in the process that they really have the greatest job there is: The Rebel Housewife! And single or married, we could all use their best Rebel Rx: Live, Love, Laugh!"

—Kimberley Kennedy, host of "Hot Topics" on Atlanta's WSB-TV

The Rebel Housewife Rules

To Heck with Domestic Bliss

SHERRI CALDWELL AND VICKI TODD

CONARI PRESS

First published in 2004 by Conari Press,
an imprint of Red Wheel/Weiser, LLC
York Beach, ME
With offices at:
368 Congress Street
Boston, MA 02210
www.redwheelweiser.com

Library of Congress Cataloging-in-Publication Data

Caldwell, Sherri.

The rebel housewife rules : to heck with domestic bliss / Sherri Caldwell and Vicki Todd.

p. cm.

ISBN 1-57324-956-4 (pbk.)

1. Family—Humor. 2. Marriage—Humor. 3. Parenting—Humor.
4. Motherhood—Humor. I. Todd, Vicki. II. Title.

PN6231.F3C35 2004

814'.6—dc22   2004007753

Typeset in Caslon
Printed in Canada
TCP
11 10 09 08 07 06 05 04
8 7 6 5 4 3 2 1

To our Cast of Characters

With all our love and heartfelt thanks—
without you, we'd have no stories.

Contents

Acknowledgments   ix
A Note to Our Readers   xi
Introduction: The Greatest Myth of All   1

PART ONE

Happily Ever After   3

CHAPTER 1   His, Mine, & Ours   5
CHAPTER 2   Training Day   9
CHAPTER 3   New Career Choices   13
CHAPTER 4   Outlaws & Other Baggage   17
CHAPTER 5   Monday Morning Flee   21
CHAPTER 6   What Did You Do All Day?   25
CHAPTER 7   The Great Escape   29
CHAPTER 8   The Fires of Passion   33

PART TWO

And Baby Makes Three   37

CHAPTER 9   No, You Are Not Ready   39
CHAPTER 10   You Get What You Get   43
CHAPTER 11   Home Is Where the Toddler Should Be   47
CHAPTER 12   Girls: Sugar & Spice, Everything Nice?   51
CHAPTER 13   Boys: You'll Always Be My Baby   55
CHAPTER 14   The Truth about Toys   59
CHAPTER 15   Reflections of Perfect Parenting   63

PART THREE

The Perfect Family   67

CHAPTER 16   Like Cats and Dogs   69
CHAPTER 17   Civil War at Home   73
CHAPTER 18   Short-Order Cook   77

CHAPTER 19   The Psychology of Money   80
CHAPTER 20   Too Much Time Together   84
CHAPTER 21   Christmas & Other Blessed Events   89
CHAPTER 22   Flying High   92

PART FOUR

Life in the Village   97

CHAPTER 23   Empty Nesters   99
CHAPTER 24   The Social Life of Moms   103
CHAPTER 25   OPMs (Other People's Monsters)   110
CHAPTER 26   It's a Strange, Strange World   114
CHAPTER 27   Making the Grade   118
CHAPTER 28   Mental Health Days   122

PART FIVE

Men, Sex, & Other Fantasies   127

CHAPTER 29   Sex, Lies, & Videotape   129
CHAPTER 30   Who Said Bigger Is Better?   134
CHAPTER 31   Things with Cords   140
CHAPTER 32   Housewife Fantasy   144
CHAPTER 33   A Whole Lotta Money, Honey   148

PART SIX

How She Does It   153

CHAPTER 34   Kahlua in My Coffee   155
CHAPTER 35   Little White Lies   159
CHAPTER 36   Mom Knows All   163
CHAPTER 37   Mommy Dearest   166
CHAPTER 38   Mom's Getaway   170

A Final Note: Keeping it All in Perspective   175
Are You a Rebel Housewife?   177
About the Authors   178

Acknowledgments

Behind every Rebel Housewife is a phenomenal support team. We wish to acknowledge the following people, with love and thanks:

Our fabulous husbands, Russ Caldwell and Brad Roos, for their constant love, encouragement, patience, and unfailing $upport in $o many way$.

Our terrific children: Zach, Haleigh, and Tiger Scott Caldwell and Clayton and Lillian Roos, for being our inspiration and motivation; for making life fun and forcing us to take time out every once in a while; and for their love, support, and enthusiastic promotion of their Rebel Housewife moms.

Our publishing team at Conari Press: Jan Johnson, Kate Hartke, Jill Rogers, and the many others who helped in the adventure of pushing this (and us) from our crazy concept to a publishing event (the first of many!).

Our faithful readers and subscribers at *www.rebelhouse wife.com*, who have believed in us, encouraged us, and responded so warmly.

And finally, all the Rebel Housewives out there, and everyone who loves them—let those wild women out of the closet and join the fun!

A Note to Our Readers

You will find two very distinct voices in the myths, realities, and rules that follow. The Rebel Housewives are Sherri Caldwell (The Redhead) and Vicki Todd (The Blonde): wives, mothers, writers, best friends, and former neighbors in Atlanta, Georgia. The strength of our friendship, and our partnership, lies in a similarity of attitude—we are both laid-back, fun, and unconventional—yet opposite personalities in many ways that may become obvious.

We thought it might be helpful to introduce our Cast of Characters up front and let you know who goes with whom in the stories and anecdotes that follow:

The Redhead & Family	**The Blonde & Family**
Sherri & Russ	Vicki & Brad
Zach	Clayton
Haleigh	Lillian
Tiger Scott (yes, that's his given name)	Lucy the Great Dane
Shaney & Data, The Mutts	Beauregard the Bunny

The Greatest Myth of All

Welcome to the Rebel Housewife experience!

We love our husbands, our children, and our roles and purpose in life as Mrs. Mom. We both chose this job. Still, as important as it is, and as rewarding as it can be—it sucks to be Mommy sometimes! If we can't have a little fun, let down our hair, laugh, commiserate, even bitch and whine once in awhile—rebel just a little—we're all in trouble!

Women, Sisters—it doesn't matter if you are older or younger, the color of your skin, whether you're married, divorced, or single—come on and join the rebellion! Our primary objectives: freedom from the trap of how we thought life *would* be; sanity; greater enjoyment of life as it really *is* . . . that's what The Rebel Housewives are all about.

We mean to dispel myths, tell it like it is, and prescribe rules to live by, with very specific action tips to help you enjoy life as a Rebel Housewife.

As a special bonus, right here in the Introduction, we are going to share the first myth with you:

The Greatest Myth of All: *By the age of thirty-five, we'll have it all figured out.*

Hello?! If you are over thirty-five, you can laugh at the naiveté

... but we believed it. We thought that when we turned thirty-five, we'd be real adults, in control and conquering the world.

By thirty-five, we'd be successfully married happily ever after to Prince Charming. We'd have our always-picture-perfect family with our two adorable children, a boy and a girl, of course. And a dog. Maybe a cat. We would live in our beautiful homes, which would always be spotless, in the suburbs, with at least two late-model cars in the garage. We were certain we'd be enjoying fulfilling careers, high-powered enough to require a great wardrobe and an expense account, yet flexible enough so that we could still be Soccer Mom, PTA President, and all-around Superwoman. . . .

Ready for reality? Some of that is true. Some of us are fortunate in finding happily-ever-after with Prince Charming . . . but it's a damn lot of work, and even Prince Charming has morning breath every day and male PMS every so often. As for the kids . . . well, let's deal with those myths, realities, and rules as we get to them! Yes, we have dogs. No cats. The spotless house, the cars . . . admit it, a minivan was never in the vision! And the career . . . oh, the career! We didn't have a clue.

As for being "real" adults, in control and conquering the world? Well, we look around and realize we *are* in charge now. It's us and all the other geeks and preppies from high school in the '80s. My, oh my. Are our kids and getting-older parents in trouble, or what?

It all comes down to the most important Rebel Housewife Rule:

The Greatest Rule of All: Live, Love, and Laugh.

One day at a time, Baby. It's a new adventure every day.

PART ONE

Happily Ever After

Chapter 7

His, Mine, & Ours

The Myth: *Combining two separate lives will be a snap.*

His, mine, and ours. United as one, isn't that in the vows? That's fine, as long as it's understood that we use my stuff. When we move into our first home together, he won't mind when I toss his college furniture. The beer-ridden futon doesn't go with my Laura Ashley décor. He will eventually learn to appreciate good wine; he won't even miss his around-the-world beer mug collection. I will need a lot of closet space, so those old college jerseys have to go.

My new husband will be so thoughtful, so in love with me. He won't care when I borrow his things, like his razor. I'm always out of blades, and I love the foaming bubbles his shaving cream makes—oh those gloriously smooth legs! Sleeping in his dress shirt feels so good; it will keep me close to him when he is out of town. Somehow I never have any socks, but not to worry, I'll just wear his.

Uniting our money will be a good thing, for there will surely be more to spend. I'll gladly let him take care of the finances. I've got a little debt coming into the union, but he won't mind. With his understanding nature and savvy financial skills, we won't even need to talk about my decision to spend my student loan on spring break in Mexico and why I'm still paying it off.

He will work hard to provide for me and our future children. He'll shower me with gifts and let me spend everything I make on myself. We'll have two separate bank accounts: his account for paying bills and spending on me, and my account, for spending on me. Seems logical.

The Reality: *His and mine don't always make ours.*

"I can't make love on a pink flowered sofa. Where's my futon?"

"I gave it to Goodwill."

"What?! I've always gotten lucky on that couch, and you threw it out?"

"How lucky?"

"Lucky with you, I mean."

We both squeezed out of that one, but when he found out I gave away his beer mugs and college jerseys, I slept alone for a week.

After I used his shaving kit, he emerged from the bathroom looking like a doctor had just removed shrapnel from his face. I felt bad, but I pretended not to notice.

"Where's my new dress shirt? I need it for an interview tomorrow."

"Ummm . . . is this the one?" I tried to look especially sexy as I pointed to what I was wearing to bed.

"Vik, come on! I have no socks, no razors, no shaving cream, nothing to drink my beer from. I have to be manly on a fluffy, pink, flowered couch and now I have nothing to wear to work!"

"It makes me feel close to you when you're gone." Sniff, sniff.

"I'm sorry, Babe. I'll find something else to wear."

It got more complicated when it came to expenses. He actually expected me to contribute! My duty was the car payment. It was shocking to see how fast the repo man comes when you forget to pay it for a few months.

I had to get a job—any job—in twenty-four hours so we could qualify for our first home. I applied for fourteen jobs in one day. I topped out at a whopping $6 an hour. This was a lot for a princess to digest—the month before, I had been trying to decide what shoes to buy with my school allowance from my parents. Home, mortgages, cars . . . couldn't we go back to the simpler days of "Dad, I need money this month"?

No, I was hitched, and in modern-day marriage, it takes two: two incomes to pay the bills. I paid my half. The rest went into savings, all 5 cents. We never got the separate accounts: He wanted to keep an eye on my spending. Can you believe he thought I would embezzle from my own husband?

In the spirit of compromise and harmony, I re-covered the sofa in green for the sake of our sex life. I found his beer mug collection on eBay and bought it back for our second anniversary.

The Rule: *Ease into combining your stuff.*

Don't play dictator. It takes two to make all parts of a marriage work, including the finances and the décor.

Rebel Rx:

1. Don't throw away his treasures without his consent.
2. Stash any new stuff you buy for a week or two, then bring it out gradually. If he asks, you can honestly say, "This old thing? No, it's just been in the closet!"
3. Before you deposit your paycheck into the joint account, take out your spending money in cash.
4. Always get cash back at the grocery store.
5. Sleep in the nude, not in his dress shirt—it saves on laundry, and he'll have something to wear to work!

Chapter 2

Training Day

The Myth: *You can turn your frog into a prince.*

We all know the honeymoon does not last forever, right? And I'm not talking about the after-the-wedding honeymoon. Lord knows, I spent one night of mine locked in the hotel bathroom, crying, "What have I done?"

Long before any vows take place, in the early days of every relationship, it's magic: We've met someone special; we think we have a lot in common; everything about the other person is fascinating, funny, adorable. The glow of infatuation, the naiveté of being young (or young at heart) and in love tends to obscure reality, for a while.

But we know best behavior doesn't last. And that's when you really get to know someone—fabulousness, faults, and all.

However, there is a Danger Zone. A myth we all fall into, to some degree. Even after the infatuation, after the honeymoon, when we've really gotten to know a person well, for better and for worse, we still think we have the power to change him:

"After the wedding . . . he'll care less about sports and hanging with the guys. . . . "

"When we have our own house . . . he'll help out more to keep it nice. . . . "

"Once we have kids . . . he'll settle down and face responsibility. . . . "

" . . . and, after, when, once, then . . . he'll be Prince Charming and we'll live happily ever after."

The Reality: *Once a frog, always a frog.*

Fundamentally, we are what we are, warts and all. If he has to hang out with the boys and crack open a beer in honor of any and all sports events before the wedding, you'll still have to put up with the friends, the beer, and the sports after the wedding. Trust me. I had our first baby on Superbowl Sunday—the new daddy's biggest concern was getting the game on the TV in the delivery room.

In fact, with a sports lover, your first big purchase will be a big-screen TV and a beer fridge. "The guys"—none of them—will ever remember to put the toilet seat down. We had to buy our first house for the TV, not for dogs or kids. And even though we bought a fixer-upper, and he had some passing enthusiasm for remodeling, we still spent more time and money at Hi-Fi Buys than at Home Depot. I ended up painting the dining room, master bedroom, and the nursery myself—six months pregnant, with an oxygen mask and my barf bucket nearby. It was, after all, football season. My best friend down the street was out mowing her lawn, nine months pregnant—her husband was out with mine at a baseball game.

Keeping the house nice: Wouldn't laundry be a great place to start? He "saves" his dirty laundry all over the bedroom and the closet, in case he needs to wear something again before "you have a chance to do laundry." Isn't that sweet? He might need to wear that raggedy old T-shirt or that one pair of jeans—the pair that is exactly like the five pairs of clean jeans in the drawer—you just never know!

And that's not even the worst of it! I admit, I'm really Type-A regarding laundry issues, but it has been *fifteen years*—and he still takes his socks and T-shirts off inside out, and never thinks to turn them right side out (before tossing them on the floor). I don't think he ever considers how it happens, when it happens, or who flips everything for him (bitching and moaning over every single sock). For a time, I thought I would gently school him, retrain him in correct laundry practices. I just stopped doing it (the flipping, not the laundry). I put the inside-out clothes in the washer, through the dryer, folded them neatly, and put them away—as is. He wore his socks and T-shirts inside-out, tags a-flapping, until I gave up and started flipping again.

It doesn't get any better when the children come along. You'd better test him with kids before things get too serious: baby-sit, spend time with nieces and nephews, go to Disneyworld . . . whatever he's like with kids before he has his own, you can get a good idea of how he will be after. Fortunately, mine had lots of good experience from being a lifeguard and a swimming instructor, and he always got along with the kids—for 45 minutes at a time, twice a week.

Still, he's a great daddy. My only complaints: They are all

little sports maniacs; my sons leave the toilet seat up, every time; and laundry skills are apparently genetic: I spend a lot of time flipping.

The Rule: *Buyer beware!*

Finding the right person is the rule. This is also the challenge. Like buying a coat, or an absolutely adorable pair of shoes that you really love—but they just don't fit. You can try all sorts of tricks and alterations; try as hard as you can. It's never going to be the same as finding exactly what you wanted, at the right time and place, for the right price. Especially when it comes to men.

Rebel Rx:

1. Trade-offs can be fun: "I'll give you putting away my hair dryer every morning . . . if you can get your dirty underwear *into* the hamper."
2. Love, consideration, and spontaneous sex go a long way toward radical (if temporary) behavioral modification.
3. Realize and appreciate: If you can live with his idiosyncrasies (all those things you thought were so cute in the beginning), he'll put up with yours, and it should all work out.
4. Don't bother with books or special courses on getting him to change—it won't work.

Chapter 3

New Career Choices

The Myth: *It's an easy street to big money.*

I made it through college, got my first job, and slowly eased my way into the workforce. After moving countless times and suffering many thankless short-term jobs, I was tired of applying and tired of getting rejected. When I did get a job, I had to work weekends and holidays. I was soon ready to retire from the traditional workforce, maybe start my own business. The possibilities were endless. With the support of my hardworking hubby, I saw dollar signs and freedom.

We were a little tight on cash, so I had to come up with a business that didn't need much capital. Pet sitting? No, I would have to work weekends. I love dogs, but I'm allergic to cats. My own retail shop? No, I would have to work weekends, and it would require too much money to start. I could go back to school—no, no chance of big money there. Think, think, think. I had to come up with an idea selling "just me" that didn't require working weekends.

I've got it! A personal trainer! I would teach women how to get and stay fit! This would be easy. All the celebrities were hiring personal trainers; suburban housewives wouldn't be far behind their idols. I loved working out; how hard could it be teaching others to do it? I could capitalize on the latest craze. I didn't want to do it alone, so I'd persuade my sister to quit her secure, big-paying job and do it with me! Together we would make loads of money, stay fit, and work from home . . . it would be Easy Street!

The Reality: *The road to riches is full of twists and turns.*

How does one become a personal trainer? I looked in the back of a magazine, found an ad for a school that provided professional certification—in a great location. I'd ask my mother for the money to get there.

Next thing I knew I was off to Maui—yes, Hawaii—with my sister, to become a personal trainer. We spent the next two months earning our certification on the sun-drenched beaches. After all that hard work for certification, we were ready for a holiday. It was our company, and we had no restrictions on vacation policy. It would be only the best for our employees, which consisted of just the two of us. We convinced my husband to come over and join us (not a hard sell). Over the "drink of the day," we all became Maui-ized and began to fantasize about dropping out of society. My husband could become a pool boy, my sister and I would be sun goddesses, and we'd all live happily ever after. . . .

Reality soon intruded. I went to use my credit card and it

was rejected. It was a rude awakening, living in Maui with no money at almost thirty. We went home so my husband could go back to his job and we could begin our new lucrative business as personal trainers.

We started our new company in debt (spent way too much money in Hawaii). No problem, we would soon have hundreds of clients. We decided to advertise in a small local newspaper. After only two days we got a client! Not just a client, but a client with a friend! We met with them and realized it was going to be a bigger job than anticipated. They had lofty goals. They wanted to lose weight fast—now!

Being optimists, and in desperate need of cash, we took on the job and even got them to pay us up front. We cashed their check (in case they changed their minds) and used the money to pay our credit cards. The first two weeks went well. We were excited when they each lost two pounds and were walking up to a mile a day. We even cooked for them. But shortly after that it went downhill. They started to cancel training sessions, complaining they were tired of eating "rabbit food" and were sick of my homegrown herbs. The results were taking too long—they showed me an ad: "Lose 10 pounds in a week and still have all you can eat!" When we asked them to renew they said *no*.

I began to have doubts about whether I'd chosen the right home business. No one else answered our ad. The accountant was on my back mumbling something about how he'd never seen so many write-offs and I was going to end up in jail if I didn't produce some income. That's okay, I had 1,001 other ideas. Just because this one didn't work didn't mean I was doomed. I can still hear my husband shouting, "No, please Vik, no more ideas! We can't afford it! Get a real job!"

The next idea was a doozer. It's time to start a family and I can still work—at home with the baby. Maybe write a book—how hard could that be?

The Rule: *Think outside the box, but be realistic.*

Choose a career you like, and don't be afraid to change your mind and try something new—it's a woman's prerogative!

Rebel Rx:

1. Find a friend to work with. It's more fun and you can split costs!
2. Don't go into debt trying to get rich quick—if it sounds too good to be true, it usually is.
3. *Warning:* Once you leave the 9 to 5 grind, there's no turning back.
4. Being your own boss has all kinds of benefits—you get to decide salaries, bonuses, and vacation policy.
5. Rebel Recommends: *Rich Dads Retire Young, Retire Rich* by Robert T. Kiyosaki (Warner Books).

Chapter 4

Outlaws &
Other Baggage

The Myth: *Marriage means one big, happy family-in-law.*

I remember meeting his family for the first time. It took days to get ready. I wanted everything to be perfect, especially me. I was so nervous, thinking these people would be part of my life forever, and I wanted them to like me.

I was willing to do whatever it took, things I would normally never consider: I oohed and aahed over Grandma's Lutefisk and choked down Aunt Jane's grape Jell-O. It didn't matter; they were soon to be my in-laws, and I wanted to make a good impression. Instead of talking, I listened. When his mom kept telling me what her son liked to eat, I took notes. I promised to remember everything. I heard all of his childhood stories: when he first walked, talked, his prom dates (how cute they were)—she left nothing out. I didn't bat an eye when Grandma tipped over in her chair. Maybe she was tired?

All I could think about was soon we would be married and our families would become one big happy family. I hoped his brothers, sisters, aunts, and uncles would rejoice that he had finally chosen the perfect wife. I knew they would be kind and supportive. I didn't think anyone would care how I planned my wedding, since it would be my day. They wouldn't object if we wanted to elope; they would shower us with wedding gifts, preferably crystal and china.

I longed to hear the words, "I think of you as my daughter; call me Mom." I had such high expectations, such high hopes for my mother-in-law. I expected her to take my side in quarrels with her son (which, of course, would be rare). My second mom would be there to hold my hand, agree with me that her son can be such a jerk sometimes, and offer advice on how to handle him during a disagreement. She would be my confidant and friend, tell me how good my hair looks and that I keep a beautiful home.

When I wanted a career and put off having grandchildren, his parents wouldn't mention my biological clock. The in-laws would respect our privacy and independence. They would call on holidays and birthdays and never, ever overstay their welcome.

The Reality: *One big family, yes. Happy, maybe not.*

When Grandma tipped over, it wasn't because she was tired—it was too many martinis! That "yummy" Lutefisk I was willing to try for love is required at all family holidays, even though only one person eats it and it smells up the house for a week.

HAPPILY EVER AFTER

When I finally had the courage to decline the grape Jell-O, another family tradition and Aunt Jane's specialty, it was a direct insult to his mom. Go figure.

With the furor among families over wedding arrangements, I'm surprised anyone makes it to the altar. The matrimonial details can cause the fangs and claws to come out between future in-laws. Who knew that grown women would get into a catfight over steak or chicken? The input from his brothers and sisters was overwhelming. Did they have to invite their third cousin's stepmother's grandmother? When we mentioned eloping, we might as well have told them we were moving to Mars. The word *elope* really got things started. His parents threatened never to visit (I wish!). They gave us a washing machine for a wedding gift, so useful. What happened to crystal and china?

I quickly learned no good can come from the words "Call me Mom." Run. There is no substitute for the one who raised you, and her loyalty stays with the one she brought into the world. Confiding in his mother was never a good idea—it only made her turn on me and blab everything to my husband. He now knows I'm not a real blonde. Okay, so he would have figured it out on his own, eventually. Comments from my second mom such as, "It's been a while since you've held a vacuum . . . I've never seen a girl eat that much . . . Do you cut you own hair?" haven't helped.

When celebrating my promotion at work, I received a gift from his parents, a rocking horse, with a note attached: "We are waiting." Waiting for what? For me to figure out what I'm going to do with a four-foot rocking horse?

The phone calls always got around to: "Why don't you ever come to Minnesota to visit?" Boy, that's a hard one: Enjoy our two week vacation in Hawaii, or spend our money going to Minnesota to stay in his childhood bedroom that hasn't changed in a quarter-century . . .

Instead, they came to visit us—and never left!

The Rule: *Along with your honey comes his family, like it or not.*

Always remember: he can talk and complain about his family, you can't.

Rebel Rx:

1. Get Caller ID.
2. Move far enough away so you can enjoy your freedom.
3. Make their travel arrangements when they plan a visit.
4. Never spill your guts to your mother-in-law.
5. Remember, everybody has a few mixed nuts in their family—he puts up with yours, you have to put up with his.

Chapter 5

Monday Morning Flee

The Myth: *He'd love to stay home with the kids all day.*

The grass is always greener, especially for parents who work outside the home. Usually (but not always!) it's Daddy who plods home at the end of the long day at work.

In a perfect world, Mommy and the kids watch for Daddy's car to come down the street on weeknights, eagerly anticipating his homecoming. The house is clean, the homework is done, a wonderful dinner is ready to eat, all together at the table. Mommy greets Daddy with a kiss and a smile. "Everything is under control here, Honey—welcome home."

He looks forward to family time at the end of the long, hard day at work. He is great with the kids—eager to hear news of the day, happy to help with homework or projects, looking forward to playing games, throwing the ball, jumping on the trampoline. He comes home early to help get the kids to their practices and activities. He clears his schedule and charges up the video camera to attend every baseball, soccer, hockey game, and dance recital. He's there for PTA meetings, teacher conferences, and school programs.

Everyone looks forward to weekends and vacations: up and out early; breakfasts together; family adventures. Get in the car and see new sights, do new things. Even just hanging around the house, cleaning out the basement, or working and playing in the yard is fun and relaxing—quality time together.

The Reality: *It's not all bonbons and soap operas.*

"You're late! I gave up an hour ago—your children are out of control."

Daddy comes home to find full-time Mommy stressed out and exhausted from a full day with the kids. The house is a disaster, she's in even worse shape, and there isn't a hint of dinner in sight, smell, or sound. He doesn't get it: All she had to do was play all day—no commute, no paperwork, no deadlines, no boss, nothing difficult. He jealously envisions her time with the kids as full of laughter and fun; daytime adventures played out by the time he gets home. If only he had time for fun, if he wasn't so tired and they weren't so noisy and annoying every night. . . . There is always somewhere to go, something to do, games, practices, events. The kids are yelling and running every which way. His wife is a basket case, trying to keep it all together—and hiding away from it all (and all of them) every chance she gets.

Weekends and vacations are particularly stressful. The kids, who can't roll out of bed on time for school during the week, are up before dawn, noisy and demanding. Dad just wants to sleep in. All of the best-laid plans for family adventure and togetherness end up in disaster—quality time is way too complicated, and the kids always want to be off doing something else, spending more money or going to McDonald's for every meal. After ten minutes in the car with them, Dad's ready to jump out.

By Sunday night, he's over Quality Time. It's time for the Monday Morning Flee. Thank God he's got an office to go to, a flight to catch. It's not all fun and games. He would not, could not stay home all day, every day with his kids. How does she do it?

Holidays and vacations are times to look forward to, but then again . . . it's always good to get back to work. The guys all admit to it—my husband told me this after one particularly high energy and stressful Christmas—they talk about it around the water cooler: "My kids are *nuts!* I can't believe how they can fight and carry on. . . . I could hardly wait to get out of the house!"

And from Mom's point of view, he gets the best of the kids and the worst of his wife at the end of a long day. He has time to play games and have fun. He doesn't have to coordinate getting everybody everywhere on time, with all their stuff; shop for groceries; prepare meals; clean house; do laundry so everybody has clean clothes and fresh sheets and towels. He doesn't get the call to pick up sick kids at school, attend teacher conferences and PTA meetings—the pressure to volunteer, to spend what little free time he has with kids! He doesn't have to drive a minivan filled with car seats and kid clutter and cart kids around to doctor and dentist appointments, all their play dates, and after-school activities. She'd do the Monday Morning Flee too, if she had the chance, but it doesn't quite work out that way.

The Rule: *Switch things around once in a while.*

Leave Daddy in charge for two or three nights every year. What you do on your Mom's Getaway is another subject (see chapter 38), but the loving appreciation your husband will have for you after handling the kids on his own will keep you going for another 362 days, especially when you can gently remind him: "You know how hard it is." Love and appreciation *and* a great excuse for the rare (?) occasion when dinner is late or he can't find any clean T-shirts.

Rebel Rx:

1. Keep up with local nanny and housekeeping rates— know how much your time is worth.
2. Have a Daddy Ritual just for them every night, or as often as possible—let Dad supervise baths or read the bedtime story.
3. Have kids e-mail Daddy news of the day.
4. Remember to have fun—all work and no play makes Mommy Dearest!

Chapter 6

What Did You Do All Day?

The Myth: *Compared to an outside career, taking care of a house and family—and myself—will be a breeze.*

Before I became a housewife, I battled it out in the real world. There were no questions about what I did all day—I worked! As a fashion buyer, I traveled to Los Angeles and New York monthly, stayed at the cozy Waldorf-Astoria, and shopped for clothes all day. My husband and I split the housework, laundry, and cooking equally. I knew what to expect. Being a productive member of society gave me confidence and self-worth.

I knew that when I decided to have children, I would stay at home and attend to the needs of my family. I thought it would go something like this:

I will enjoy every square foot of my highly organized, superclean house. With my perfect home always so effortlessly clean, I'll have time to go to the gym and stay in tip-top shape; time to volunteer at the homeless shelter and give blood twice a week. I will enjoy spending hours in my children's classes at school: I'll be class mom *and* head of the parent group! I'll even have time to work in my garden, growing fresh fruits and vegetables to feed my family every night. The kids will love everything green.

With the little snug bugs fast asleep by seven, I will relish my nightly ritual of ironing their clothes, making their school lunches, and let's not forget, organizing each days' memories in the scrapbook. Before I lay my head down to sleep on freshly ironed sheets, I'll take in a couple of chapters of a good book to enrich my mind and then put on a sexy negligee and give my husband all the wild passionate sex he wants.

The Reality: *The daily plan changes even before you've finished making one.*

"Wow, the house is a disaster. What did you do all day?"

I growl, "What do you mean, 'What did I do all day?'" I unplugged four toilets while doing five loads of laundry, the direct result of our daughter changing her clothes ten times a day. Next, the phone rang: It was the school calling to tell me our daughter was sick and needed to come home. I got in the car and drove to school, convinced she's faking (again). I attempted a quick trip through the grocery store on the way home. She threw up on me while I was hovering over the produce. I managed to get through Starbucks drive-thru for a double venti latte, but not fast enough before she vomited again. When we got home, I put her to bed with a bucket, cleaned up the car, and got back to the laundry. I doused everything with wrinkle remover to forego the ironing, sure my grandmother was turning over in her grave. I placed three baskets of clean laundry on the stairs to be put away tomorrow or sometime this century.

Time to pick up the other child. I dragged the sick one out of bed, still clutching the bucket, and got her in the car, careful to prop her up with towels for easier cleanup. I ran back into the house to grab my lifeline—my cell phone—so I could dial a friend to commiserate about the day's events while I waited in the car pool line. After car pool, I was subjected to my six-year-old son with the "I Need Syndrome." (An expensive syndrome for which the only cure is buying him whatever he's whining about so he will shut up.)

I endured two hours of baseball practice with the sick child in the car, freezing my patootie off while trying to throw pitches to the boys. My cell phone rang. My husband: "Hi Honey! I'll be home early."

"What?!" I gathered up my son and all his stuff, left baseball early to start "The Instant Tornado." The Instant Tornado is when you throw everything and anything into a closet to make your house look clean, all the while threatening the kids with "Santa Claus won't bring you any toys if you don't bathe quickly while I make you dinner!"

Oh no, what dinner? I had to leave the grocery store with the vomiting child. I rummaged through the freezer and pulled out some leftover BBQ for hubby, while playing short-order cook for the kids: PB&J with raisins on the side.

I marched the troops to bed for our bedtime reading of Barbies and Dinosaurs. I gave each child 10,000 kisses and said goodnight.

I wondered why the dog was pacing around me, and then remembered I forgot to feed her this morning. Oops. I scooped out some frozen BBQ with the dog food and begged forgiveness. I thawed out the rest of the BBQ to create some kind of meal with it, while dreaming about foregoing dinner to hop into bed and just sleep.

My husband comes home to a disheveled wife, a disaster of a house, and laundry all over the stairs:

"What did you do all day?"

The Rule: *Be proud of your most important accomplishments: your kids. They won't remember what they had for supper.*

There is not a lot of free time in a mom's day. If you have something planned, something else always comes up. There are days when I have it all together, but most of the time I just wing it. Staying at home will never be like battling it out in the working world, but moms learn how to be spontaneous, flexible, and resourceful—qualities that are just as important to survival.

Rebel Rx:

1. Limit kids' extracurricular activities to avoid the dreaded Chauffer Syndrome (being in the car all day). Sign the kids up with friends and neighbors so you can take turns driving.

2. Practice the "Instant Tornado"; it is a critical skill.

3. Start Happy Hour early on Fridays. It works for Sherri and me!

Chapter 7

The Great Escape

The Myth: *The Romantic Weekend Getaway.*

Aaaahhhh . . . to escape with Prince Charming from the house, the kids, the everyday life; a chance to get in touch with each other, without all the interruptions and distractions; sweet freedom to enjoy being adults, husband and wife instead of Mommy and Daddy; to be able to relax without constant demands (from kids, anyway) for food, potty breaks, guidance, and attention.

What do you do with do-whatever-you-want grown-up time? Make sweet, sweet love, of course! Plenty of that—anytime, anywhere—along with carousing, fine dining, leisurely shopping, dancing, and nightlife without a care in the world.

Of course you'll call every night, just to check in, make sure everything is all right. Your children will be so happy to hear from you, so happy that you are off relaxing and having a good time. . . .

The Reality: *You're too pooped to party.*

Nothing else causes such uproar, such anguish, intense pre-planning, strategizing, and guilt. Before you even get out the door, you're stressed out and exhausted from all the preparations to make sure everything and everyone is provided for and taken care of, with an hour-by-hour schedule with phone numbers, emergency contacts, and medical release forms for anyone and everyone who might come in contact with your children and might have to take them to the hospital while you are gone. The laundry is done, meals planned and plenty of food put up, the house is clean, and you are off. . . .

By the time you get where you are going, all you want to do is sleep!

Make love? Okay, that can be relaxing, and it's a good way to start, but then let's shower, get dressed, and go out for a nice dinner and dancing. We'll go for a long walk under the moonlit stars and talk romance, stay up until dawn and have champagne with breakfast! Hmmm . . . maybe we should just snuggle for a few minutes, take a little nap so we can stay up all night . . . and there we both were when we woke up the next morning, the first night of our Romantic Weekend Getaway, slept away!

The next day we decide to take it easy and lounge around the pool in the sun, which is nice, except for one little problem: OPMs. We took all the time and trouble to get away from our own kids, only to be surrounded by Other People's Monsters!

Of course, by the end of the long day of relaxing, with maybe a walk or a game of golf to break things up, it's back to the room to get ready for dinner and The Big Night Out—this is it, don't lie down! And all we do over dinner is talk about the kids. We actually start to *miss* them.

We call to check in: big mistake. They were fine, having fun, not even thinking about us; now they are crying and want us to come home. *Now.* We appease them with promises we'll bring home presents, which becomes our primary objective the next day.

When we go out dancing, it's noisy and crowded and expensive, too. We escape for the quiet walk in the moonlight, which is nice. The promise of wild, passionate sex is fulfilled, but it's never the all-night affair or the marathon sessions we enjoyed in our younger days, B.C. (Before Children). Still, we don't have to worry about being too noisy (we don't know any of these people!); nobody walked in on us; and I woke up the next morning naturally—one beautiful Sunday morning when I was not blasted out of sleep by the ear-piercing screams of children up far too early, fighting over cereal and television programs. I turned to my husband for a late-morning snuggle. We'd have to be up and out soon to make the 11:00 A.M. check-out and get home to the kids—and we still had to find souvenirs!

The Rule: *Be realistic in your expectations.*

Plan a full day to unwind before play begins. Add to your list of things to do simple, elegant, truly relaxing pleasures like a long bubble bath, a good massage (professional or otherwise!), and a good book. Don't wear yourself out trying to relax!

Rebel Rx:

1. Enjoy long car trips together with conversation and books on tape, or go X-rated: Read *Penthouse* Forum stories out loud to him while he drives—you'll both be in the mood when you get there.

2. Don't call home, and don't leave a number—that's the beauty of cell phones: they can reach you if they need to.

3. Secret tip: To avoid OPMs, stay at adult resorts.

4. Sometimes the greatest escape is to stay home—send the kids away!

Chapter 8

The Fires of Passion

The Myth: *Happily ever after is hot, Hot, HOT!*

Romance. Passion. Marriage. More romance, more passion
. . . it just continues, effortlessly.

There are actually two versions of this myth:

Version 1: The promise of the wedding vow. It's just that
simple to love, honor, and cherish "as long as you both shall
live." Of course that means sex too! Guilt-free, safe, uncom-
plicated sex-on-request, whenever, wherever. If you can, why
wouldn't you?

The ultimate promise of marriage is a love and passion
that grows every day and deepens through the years, encom-
passing the birth of children and the natural progression of
life:

Through the excitement of the twenties: "Let's have *sex!*"

The growth of the thirties: "Let's make love . . . this weekend."

The stability of the forties: "The kids are gone for the night—let's have sex!"

The empty nesting of the fifties: "Let's make love . . . on the kitchen table!"

The retirement of the sixties: "Let's have sex on the road—get in the RV!"

The grandparenting of the seventies: "???"
And who knows what lies beyond that . . .?

Version 2, the one I was familiar with as I was growing up: Eventually companionship and shared history take precedence over passion. "You grow out of the need for all the other stuff." (What?!) My grandparents had separate bedrooms from my earliest memories (their fifties)—and there were no sleepovers. That's just the way it was. They loved each other, but they didn't spend much time together during the day, none at all at night. No passion. "That's just what happens."

The Reality: *You have to add fuel to the fire to keep it going.*

Thank goodness I eventually gained some exposure to sixty-, seventy-, and eighty-year-olds outside of my own family! I have seen dynamic, loving, passionate relationships well into the sunset of life—"old" people having fun and doing things I can't even imagine having the energy for, and I'm only thirty-something! (It's the having young children that does it to you, more so than the years.)

Effortlessly? No. The marriage ceremony is so innocent, so sweet, so optimistic—that's the easy part. The honeymoon is over by the end of the first year, and you start thinking, "That's *it?* That's the only person I'll ever have sex with, ever again?"

Come on. Having sex with the same person gets boring, monotonous, ho-hum. And with the added complications of kids, careers, stress, and exhaustion . . . Good God! No wonder so many people divorce or go outside the marriage for sexual fulfillment. (Stay with me for a minute, I am not advocating anything other than monogamy—read on!)

Having been through it (and survived, thankfully!), I *know* why there is a "seven year itch": you've been there, done that enough times to know oh-so-familiar territory; all pretense is off, and you've both burped, farted, and thrown up in front of each other. Most likely you've had a kid or two, and with the current incomprehensible popularity of the "Family Bed," you probably have at least one child crowded up between you every night. What's a Rebel Housewife to do?

The Rule: *Work it, Girl!*

Marriage, and intimate time, must be a priority—for both of you. The kids will grow up and (eventually) move out, and you'll be stuck with each other—sweet freedom! You have to keep it fun, sexy, and exciting—even after decades together, even after the exhaustion of working and parenting and just getting through each day.

When you get bored with each other—change! Do something different. Be creative. Surprise each other. If you make the effort, he will too.

Rebel Rx:

1. Have an affair, if you must. Just be sure it's with your husband! It's a lot safer, easier, less expensive, and can be *really* fun!

2. Send him spicy e-mail, or distract him during the day with an X-rated text message on his pager or cell phone.

3. Make lunch dates, a.k.a. "nooners." Have a nice lunch . . . or whatever!

4. Play and have fun: dress up (or down), fantasize, make believe, surprise him with toys and props, as simple as whipped cream, or . . . !

5. There are few men alive who wouldn't be excited to receive a brown paper- or black plastic-wrapped magazine or fun package in the mail. Surprise = Fun!

PART TWO

And Baby Makes Three

Chapter 9

No, You Are Not Ready

The Myth: *Having a baby is easy—it's all in the preparation.*

I was ready. I spent months toiling over which crib to buy, weeks picking out the bedding. Should it be the cuddly little bears or the teeny-tiny racing cars? I hand-washed all the little clothes with hypoallergenic, perfume-free organic soap. I painstakingly ironed every itsy-bitsy nightshirt. The gentle sound of pitter-patter and cooing filled my dreams. I could almost smell the sweetness of freshly bathed baby—Mustela baby care products, of course; $30 a bottle, but nothing would be too good for my baby.

My bundle of joy would be the picture of perfection, wearing that one-of-a-kind hand-knit onesie with the 30 buttons and matching beaded booties. He would love to eat my home-made baby food. He would of course sleep all night, so my husband and I could have more great sex to produce more perfect children.

My new best friend was the saleswoman at the Right Start; I hung on her every word. I stocked up on learning toys, safety devices, talking Barneys, and let's not forget the all-important parenting books. I read them from cover to cover; I was prepared for everything.

I would be the Perfect Mom, maybe even get a job in my spare time. I would workout, get back in shape immediately, and all the while maintain a June Cleaver home. What could be so hard about caring for an infant?

The Reality: *Baby changes everything. There is no way to prepare.*

Cry, cry, cry, poop, poop, poop. Shower . . . what's that?! I'm not sure why I worried over his bedding; he never saw it and still (seven years later) seems to prefer mine. He spit up my home-made green peas on the hand-knit baby outfit in the first five minutes. I couldn't get it unbuttoned. After thirty minutes of scrubbing, it fell apart and the beads ended up all over the floor. Of course, the green pea stain is still there.

The all-natural soap produced an ugly circle-shaped rash over his bum. The little angel found the $30 bottle of Mustela and squeezed it out on the floor; the dog seemed to like it. I moved on to Suave—hey, it smells good! Of course my bundle of joy sleeps all night, right between me and his father. As far as that sex thing . . . I never expected we would have an audience.

Is there ever time to consult the parenting books? I have discovered that their sole purpose is to torture me with my own inadequacies, and my mother can do that. I now have many part-time jobs: Nanny, Housekeeper, Chef, Laundry Mistress. (And yes, this Laundry Mistress has ended her affair with the iron!)

I am 100 percent positive that *Shape* magazine should count walking from one end of the house to the other doing the "deep-knee-bend baby shuttle dance" a workout.

Somehow all those months preparing seem kind of . . . well . . . a waste of time!

The Rule: *You'll never be ready for life A.C. (after childbirth).*

Instead of wasting all that precious pregnancy time and money buying, reading, and preparing baby stuff that you'll never use, spend some of that time and money on yourself! It may be a while before you have a little self-indulgent luxury again.

Rebel Rx:

1. Buy yourself a sparkly bauble; let everyone else buy for the baby.
2. Schedule a pedicure one week before your due date. At least your toes will be beautiful when you can see them again!
3. Never buy newborn-sized clothing. You will get enough as gifts, and baby will outgrow them about a week *before* birth.

4. Enjoy the last days of your pregnancy, as miserable and uncomfortable as they may be: It's much easier to sleep, feed, care for, and carry that baby around on the *inside* than on the *outside*.

Chapter 10

You Get
What You Get

The Myth: *You have procreative control.*

There once was a naïve young couple who thought they could control the natural universe, or at least their own very small part of it. They thought they had some degree of choice and control, some measure of influence regarding their biological offspring. They thought, since everything else in their lives together had been fairly smooth sailing, that they could plan and organize and schedule having and bringing up children—they could continue having everything their own way: perfect.

Of course, the couple knew, from their own experiences growing up, once kids reach their teenage years, all bets were off—they would be lost, as far as any meaningful influence. But they believed strongly in the concept of the "formative" years, that brief period of time when they would have total control and could teach their children and bring them up in their own ideal—no television, no sugar, no fast food, love of classic art, literature, and music—before sending them out into the cold, cruel world. After all, if you teach a child well and ingrain good habits, they'll stick to them, even through those rebellious teenage years. Right?

Certainly before the baby's birth, the couple could predetermine many factors through proper prenatal diet, exercise, labor and delivery and parenting classes. They would know the sex of the baby. They would choose the ideal name and decorate the nursery to perfection—environment affects so many things, you know! They could even preprogram music and language preferences in utero with good tapes and a quality set of headphones! They would be ready to handle every detail competently. There would be no surprises, no crises, since things like that could only happen if you were not prepared.

Even before conception, there were many details that could be worked out. This naïve young couple thought they could choose whether their baby would be a boy or a girl. They decided their child would be a boy. They read and studied the issue and discovered all kinds of "scientific" research, advice, and old wives' tales. They enthusiastically set about to make a boy—it was all about temperature, scheduling, timing, and position. It was actually a lot of fun!

The Reality: *Life is full of surprises.*

It took a little longer than they expected, but eventually the

AND BABY MAKES THREE

couple achieved success—the stick turned blue! But that only meant they were pregnant; they had to wait several months to confirm the sex of the baby.

The day finally arrived when they were scheduled for the ultrasound, when the doctor could finally confirm for them that a baby boy was on his way. Of course, as long as the baby was healthy—that's the most important thing. But they knew he would be: they were being so careful to follow the perfect regimen of diet, exercise, plenty of rest; they were on schedule with all of the prenatal education; they read to the bump and played classical music and foreign language tapes through high-quality stereo headphones strapped around Mom's belly.

The doctor checked all the vital statistics and then all the important measurements—the baby was healthy and everything was just right. But they were having trouble getting the money shot: The baby was all curled up sleeping and they couldn't tell if that baby had a penis or not. The doctor said it would have to be a surprise—I said, "No way!" (You knew it was me all along, didn't you?) I had to know. I was terrified of having a girl. I had convinced myself, and my husband, that I was a "boy-mom." I would have no idea how to bring up a girl, what to do with a girl: all the buttons and bows and cute little dresses with tights; much less raising a girl through puberty, adolescence, and the whole future wedding nightmare. . . .

In a panic, I told the doctor, "You fire that machine back up and poke and prod this baby until you find his penis!"

Unfortunately, the penis was never found—"he" was very much a she, and we had a daughter. My husband took me to lunch, and I cried. All the best-laid plans, all the timing and scheduling and having sex doggie-style (that was supposed to be the boy-making position) . . . well, actually, it's not like any of that was a waste of time . . . but a girl? Could the ultrasound be wrong?

And what about all the rest of it? The pregnancy regimen, the formative years? All the influence and control we were supposed to have over our offspring? It was a rude awakening for the young, naïve couple . . . the first of many, as it turned out. (They were happy and excited to have a healthy, baby girl . . . once the shock wore off.)

The Rule: *You get what you get and you don't pitch a fit.*

It took us five years to come across this easy rule. Appropriately enough, it was our daughter who brought home this simple, reassuring concept, the classroom wisdom of her kindergarten teacher. For recovering perfectionists, it's the first step in The Program: words to live by—especially the moment you decide to have children. You get what you get and you don't pitch a fit.

Rebel Rx:

1. Get it embroidered on a pillow, painted on a wall, lipsticked on a mirror—whatever you need to keep it in front of you.

2. Be open to the adventure and surprise of life. Relax and have fun, since you have very little control anyway.

3. Get over being organized and prepared—that's only for people without kids!

Chapter 11

Home Is Where the Toddler Should Be

The Myth: *Toddlers are so adorable, they are welcome everywhere.*

Oh, here comes little Johnny! Look how sweet he is; I love toddlers! Look at him try to walk; he just waddles back and forth on those cute, chubby little legs banging into tables. He's so good, everyone loves when I bring him with me. He's a mama's boy and I can't leave him at home. I don't trust a sitter, and when I leave him with Grandma, he cries so hard; she tells me he's fine after I leave, but I don't believe her.

The barbeque at Vicki's was a blast! They don't have kids yet, so she and Brad enjoy the time they get to spend with Johnny. I was the only one who brought my kid—lucky I did, he was so entertaining! I never laughed so hard as when he threw 1,000 rocks into the pool and then cried when no one would fetch them. Brad was a good sport about trying to fish them out; that entertained our little precious for an hour. That old vase should have never been on the glass table; it could have hurt him when he was crawling around. It's lucky Johnny didn't get cut when it broke!

They could have been a little more thoughtful and had some kid snacks for him, but I think I forgot to tell them I was bringing him. It's okay—he seemed to enjoy the blueberry cobbler, even though it was a tad bit messy. It got his new shirt all dirty, so I had to take it off, but I just picked him up, lowered his chubby, naked body into the pool and dipped him like I was doing the wash. He loved it—especially the purple swirls in the water! Unfortunately, he ate all the cobbler so the adults didn't have any dessert.

John, Sr., had a few too many beers (we haven't been out in a while), the crowd went wild when he sang "They call it the streak!" while Johnny ran around the backyard naked with a golf club making divots everywhere. It was entertainment for everyone. The peeing on the deck might have been a little much, but I'm sure everyone understands, he's just a *baby!*

It's just too bad he wouldn't go to bed (he's not used to going to sleep on a king-sized bed). I'm surprised they don't have any type of toddler bed for guests. My poor baby was up past midnight. It makes him grumpy the next day to be up that late. I hope next time we visit they will be more prepared!

The Reality: *Toddlers are like puppies: cute and entertaining for a few minutes; then everyone wishes you would put them back in their kennel.*

AND BABY MAKES THREE

We need new friends! Friends without kids, or friends who know how to get a sitter! Can you imagine bringing a toddler over for dinner and not asking! That was the worst night—I worked so hard to prepare for the dinner party. Three days preparing the duck, for what: to serve duck à la burnt! And I can't believe the child ate the entire blueberry cobbler; and then ran his grimy little hands all over the upholstered furniture to wipe them off!

I have heard enough! "Little Johnny this, little Johnny that . . . Isn't he cute when he runs around naked?"

No, he is not cute peeing in my flowers. He killed them, and I nurtured them from seeds. Our yard looks like the gopher from *Caddyshack* paid a visit.

"Please don't light the candles; little Johnny might get hurt."

Well then, leave him at home for the safety of everyone! Have they never heard of ambiance? The crawling around the dinner table in his diaper was the topper—hygiene at its finest! The nerve of Janet, letting him play with my great-grandmother's vase and accusing me of not having a "child-safe house" when he broke it! Where did she expect him to sleep—don't they schlep beds with them? Did he have to go under my custom-made silk duvet and matching sheets with a leaky sippy cup? The purple grape juice stains just don't come out. It ended up being a $2,000 dinner party with all that destruction!

The Rule: *Bring your toddler to an adult party only when he's been invited.*

As a new parent, you will have many life-altering experiences you will want to share with everyone, but not everyone wants to share your precious jam-eater with you! Enjoy taking your toddler to appropriate places, like play dates with other toddlers, the playground, et cetera—an adult dinner party is not one of them.

Rebel Rx:

1. Hey, Grandma raised you, right? Let her take care of little Johnny and give you and your husband a break.

2. Keep some adult time for you and your husband and your childless friends. It's good to get away from baby for a couple of hours.

3. Don't lose your identity completely—no one wants to listen to an adult talk baby talk all night, and it's not good for your brain to sing nursery rhymes all day, every day—get out! Read a newspaper, or watch something PG.

4. If you were invited to bring your child, make sure you have all the essentials—toys, food, Pack n' Play, bedding. It will make everyone more comfortable.

Chapter 12

Girls: Sugar & Spice, Everything Nice?

The Myth: *The sweet, temperate nature of girls.*

Consider visions of crisp pinafores and hair bows, adorable faces and clean hands. Girls are so much easier, quieter, and nicer than boys. Girls smell better. Girls find their little soul sisters and settle into friendships for life. You never have to worry about girls at play.

Boys tend to be noisy, dirty, and wild. Things get broken when boys are around. Boys, even in play, are rough and tumble. When they aren't playing, disagreements are knock-down, drag-out fights, bruises and bleeding. Small animals hide, younger children run . . . boys are trouble. And if two boys playing together suddenly get very quiet, you'd better run to find out what mischief they are up to, before too much damage is done.

Girls have quiet interests: arts and crafts, dress-up, fairy tales, playing house, let's pretend. They are naturally more caring and compassionate. Girls love animals and babies. Whenever something happens—something gets broken, a mess is made, somebody gets hurt, it's natural to assume it was a boy. Guilt by gender.

If that's true, who (almost) killed the bunny?

The Reality: *Wild, wonderful, modern girls.*

Vicki and I both have sons and daughters the same ages. We frequently kid-swap to separate squabbling siblings—the boys go to one house to play, the girls go to the other, and it works out great. One quiet Sunday, the girls went to Vicki's and the boys played together at my house. Late in the afternoon, we exchanged back. I was happy to report the boys had been terrific—had mostly played outside all afternoon, no trouble. Vicki was ecstatic with the girls; they had been so good, so quiet, playing down in the basement playroom.

Minutes later, I got a frantic call from Vicki—there was something wrong with Beauregard, their pet bunny, who enjoys a life of relative luxury in his pen down in the basement. He wasn't moving, and there was rabbit fur all over the basement. Had the dog been down there and gotten into the rabbit cage? No, Lucy had been upstairs all day. . . . What had the girls done to the bunny?

Haleigh and Lillian are best friends for life, soul sisters—they are the only six-year-old girls who can put up with each other for any length of time. Most other little girls are far too sweet and acquiescent for our strong-willed little Amazons. They manage to get along fairly well together, probably because neither takes any crap from the other—and I don't think they ever really listen to each other. Minute-to-minute and hour-by-hour they go back and forth, sometimes fighting and bitching at each other, but whenever I jump in and suggest maybe it's time to go home, I get the tragic, horrified *"No!"* in stereo. They love each other so, they can't stand to be apart. . . .

However, that afternoon, upon interrogation and cross-examination by their respective mothers, they turned on each other in an instant (as only women can do): "It was all her idea—I told her to stop! I didn't do anything!"

Eventually, all the horrible details came out, and we managed to piece together the pathetic series of unintentional tortures those girls inflicted on the poor rabbit, in the name of "play": he was the baby; he was "skating" on the air hockey table; he was playing post office with them, and, as "the letter," he got shoved through the steps on the slide a couple of times (granted, it's a fairly wide opening). No wonder he wasn't moving—he was thoroughly exhausted. We hoped that's all it was.

Vicki stayed up all night with poor Beauregard, and took him to the vet the next morning. Fortunately, he wasn't seriously injured, but he stayed overnight with the vet for observation. Vicki and I debated back and forth appropriate consequences and punishment, and ended up deciding the girls would go with her to the veterinary hospital to bring Beauregard home. She called ahead so the vet would be ready to talk to the girls about cruelty to animals, even if it had been unintentional. That discussion had a huge impact on the girls, and while I would say they are "nicer," especially to small animals, I still wouldn't go so far as to say "everything" nice. I'm sure the bunny would agree.

The Rule: *Always be suspicious if things get too quiet—boys or girls.*

In these modern times, self-esteem, self-confidence, positive self-image, and self-acceptance will get our girls a lot further than always being "nice." While it can be challenging to raise a strong-willed girl, we have to appreciate and foster that inner strength which will serve them well as self-reliant, independent women.

Rebel Rx:

1. Make a habit of talking—and, more important, listening—to your daughter.
2. Girls need exposure to a wide spectrum of friends and activities to develop their own interests and identities.
3. *Caution:* Know your daughter's friends. Do everything you can to keep her out of groups and cliques that can be harmful to her self-image.
4. Set a good example by being your own unique, strong, independent woman—*Girl Power!*
5. Rebel Recommends: *Odd Girl Out: The Hidden Culture of Aggression in Girls* by Rachel Simmons (Harcourt).

Chapter 13

Boys: You'll Always Be My Baby

The Myth: *Once you're "Mom," you'll never be "Mommy" again.*

As far as gender stereotyping, we've come a long way in the last thirty years. You will occasionally see a boy in ballet or gymnastics, and there are more male nurses and teachers; maybe a few male hair stylists and designers who are not gay. Still, it seems to be more the exception than progressive acceptance for men to be in touch with their softer side.

Men and boys still tend, indeed are generally encouraged, toward the male model of action versus words; aggression versus passivity; rational versus emotional; GI Joe versus Barbie; and independence. Big boys don't cry. They don't run to their mommies. A girl is your daughter, and will be for life; a boy is your son until he has a wife.

The Reality: *It's "Mom" in public, still "Mommy" at home.*

I knew the time would come when my son would no longer appreciate my enthusiastic mothering and public displays of affection. I promised myself I would respect his need for independence when the time came.

I enjoyed all the snuggling and closeness I could get when he was young and still in love with his mommy. I never minded getting up with him in the middle of the night to have that quiet, special time together. I cherished each time I could use my mommy-magic to kiss a boo-boo and make it all better. I loved seeing his little face light up when he saw me every morning, and I treasured all those precious little boy hugs and kisses.

He was six years old when he started calling me Mom; when he started being more excited about a play date with a friend than time with Mom; when he turned his face away in embarrassment when I kissed him good-bye at school. It wasn't long before I started getting The Rules:

"Mo-ommm, don't hug me in front of everyone."

"Mo-ommm, I can't hold your hand!"

"Mo-ommm, don't talk baby-talk! It's my stomach."
(I had inadvertently told the doctor he had a "tummy ache.")

It is true: Boys reach the age of fierce separation and independence sooner than you are ready, but here's the good news: All that pushing away, all The Rules—that's only in public!

For a couple more years at least, in the privacy of your own home or when it is just you and him, he still snuggles!

My big, fiercely-independent-kid-by-day is the first one to sit on my lap to watch TV or read a bedtime story, which he still wants me to read out loud to him. He insists on being properly tucked in every night, complete with hug and kiss. He actually likes seeing me at school, loves it when I can have lunch with him and his friends. I am careful not to embarrass him—I know The Rules. We haven't teased him about girls or crushes since kindergarten, when we learned teasing is a huge mistake: He stopped talking to me for a week when I told his secrets. But as long as you're cool—he'll keep talking.

One of his new favorite books at bedtime (in between the boy-hero adventures of Harry Potter and Artemis Fowl) is a sappy little story we received as a gift when he was first born: *Love You Forever* by Robert Munsch. For years, I stopped reading this one because it made me cry every time I read it to him. It's about a mother and son growing older; the mom always tucked her son in at night, even sneaking into his house after he became an adult to tell him, "I'll love you forever, I'll like you for always, As long as I'm living my baby you'll be." I couldn't take it, but I couldn't throw the book away, and he found it on his shelf. He *loves* this book and makes me read it all the time: "Read the one that makes you cry, Mom." I still break down into the boo-hoos every time.

One of the best moments of my day is when I turn off the light and say, "Good night, Zach. I love you." He still responds, "Good night. I love you, too, Mom."

The Rule: *Take it while you can get it!*

Fully indulge in and enjoy every moment of your precious mommy-time, with both boys and girls. You have to respect their need for separation and independence, and eventually let them go, but you may have more time than you think. In private, anyway.

Rebel Rx:

1. Follow the rules that are important to your son. Be perceptive.
2. Never push your son away when he needs you. Keep him talking by letting him know you are listening.
3. Resist the urge to tease or embarrass your son, especially about girls or showing emotion.
4. Always remember: You are the first love of your son's life, the standard by which all other women will be judged. Do right by your future daughter-in-law!

Chapter 14

The Truth about Toys

The Myth: *There is no such thing as too many toys.*

Before I had children, I assumed toys were a good thing. I would wander around FAO Schwartz and get a warm, fuzzy feeling with the anticipation of one day being able to buy my children the big giraffe—you know the one, it stands six feet tall. I loved to run my fingers through the ultra-soft bear rug and tiptoe on the piano mat that plays music. I didn't think it was possible for a child to have too many toys. I never thought I had enough! I could hardly wait to have children, to buy them all the toys I dreamed of as a child and more.

There are toys for everything: toys to teach kids to play, toys to aid in sleeping, toys for the senses, and the ultimate: educational toys. There is a happy green frog that teaches kids to read. And if he fails, you can rely on Barney the purple dinosaur. He interacts with your child by singing and dancing so you don't have to. There is the talking globe that will make them a whiz at geography. Just in case anything is missed by the frog, the dinosaur, and the globe, you can count on the endless variety of computer games to make up any deficiency. A child hardly needs to go to school anymore with all these advancements.

My son gets so excited when he sees a TV commercial for a new toy. It's always the latest, greatest thing, immediately superseding whatever was latest and greatest the minute before. The battery-operated dog looks so real: All the fun of a dog, but no doo doo to clean up. How wonderful for the parents—one less mess! Toy manufacturers always have the parents in mind, not only in marketing so strenuously to our little angels; they make the toys so durable, so easy—unpack and play, instant happiness.

The Reality: *Toys will ruin your life.*

What was I thinking? I should be sent to the loony bin. Why did I buy so many? One learning block set was not enough; I had to buy ten other toys as well. Who did I think was going to put away all those toys? Where did I think I was going to fit that stupid giraffe? It takes up the entire room, and I always step on the piano just when I've got them finally asleep.

It's not just me who overindulges the kids. Grandpa and Grandma are guilty too. Instead of buying them one toy at Christmas, they buy them ten; ten breakable toys that have to be assembled and then, immediately upon completion, fall apart. Kids don't even have to wait until their birthday or Christmas anymore. These days, they get toys and prizes for every occasion: a trip to the dentist, a haircut, even with meals!

We are forced into buying the educational toys through guilt and fear. You begin to believe if you don't have them all, your child will end up being a dummy. Every time my daughter goes to play with the Barney doll, he needs new batteries and his words come out like he had one too many martinis. The frog who teaches reading is even more annoying than Barney, and the globe just plain stinks. The letters of the states are so small we can't read them, and every time you touch a state with the magic pen, it gives the wrong answer. My son is going to think the capital of Maine is New York! The computer games do nothing more than turn my kids into video zombies.

That talking, walking, battery-operated dog—the one that looked so real on TV—when I got it home, finally got it free of the packaging, got it assembled, got the batteries in, and set it on the floor, it instantly fell apart and so did my son. Do you know it takes half an hour to get one Barbie out of her packaging? They keep her from escaping with tiny screws and plastic straps and stitch her hair to the box! Those little screws should be banned. Screwing Barbie to cardboard seems so inhumane—even for a plastic doll. When she was finally released from her bondage, I yanked too hard, and her ensemble flew all over the floor. I lost one of those miniature shoes, which sent my daughter into a tizzy—can't they glue them to her feet? They've done everything else to the poor girl!

The Rule: *Manage your children's toys early on.*

Make rules with friends and family: Don't buy more than one; no batteries; givers must assemble their own gifts; and gifts should be given only for birthdays and Christmas.

Rebel Rx:

1. Out with an old toy to bring in a new one!
2. Don't let the kids watch TV—commercials will make everyone miserable.
3. Hide the ads from the Sunday paper, and toss all mail-order catalogs.

Chapter 15

Reflections of Perfect Parenting

The Myth: *We can create super children with our parenting skills.*

Parents are lauded for the success and damned for the failures of their children. A child is, after all, the direct reflection of his or her parents. It's all up to Mom and Dad: how the kid looks, acts, and smells; her IQ, where he goes to school; his athletic ability, or lack thereof. Ever see a scruffy kid? What's the first thing that comes to mind? The parents, of course! Why don't they bathe her? Why is his shirt not clean? It's all about the parents and how they raised him or her; the child is innocent.

In theory, if you go the extra mile as a parent, you will see the positive results in your children. Think of the possibilities! There are lessons, tutors, flash cards, computer software, and books for all your needs. You can train him to read by two, learn a second language by three, captain the baseball team by four, and send him off to a prestigious kindergarten by five—unless the little genius skips preschool and moves right on to first grade.

You can be sure all the time and energy will pay off down the road. When he's not playing major league baseball in the off-season, he will be attending an Ivy League university (on scholarship maybe?), which will ensure his financial success, which will result in his marrying the perfect wife, fathering 2.5 perfect children and leading a perfectly happy life, which will all reflect so well on you!

The Reality: *You can only do so much.*

"Strike one . . . Strike two! . . . Steee-rike *three*—you're *out!*"

"My god, he struck out again! How can he do that? I never struck out as a kid. I was an awesome baseball player. He's the only kid on the team that strikes out."

"He's having fun, right?"

"Yeah, but he's making me look bad!"

Why, when my mother comes to visit, does my son choose to wear the red polka-dot T-shirt (the dots added by me and my handy dandy bleach bottle) that is three sizes too small? I see the look she gives him . . . and then me.

"Does Clayton need new clothes for his birthday? Maybe a haircut too."

My aunt is convinced I didn't comb my daughter's hair for the first four years of her life. I tried, I really tried. Every morn-

AND BABY MAKES THREE

ing she screamed while I squirted an entire bottle of detangler on her head and brushed it smooth—an hour later it was back to the rat's nest. I threw in the towel—and the detangler—and learned to live with it.

In order not to repeat history—I was kicked out of the church choir at six for singing too loudly and out of tune—I enrolled my daughter in voice lessons. The only lesson learned was that the voice fairy skipped the women in my family—I demanded a refund.

Occasionally, I have trouble remembering I'm not supposed to use profanity around children. I find this a hard habit to break. When Clayton came home with a note from the French teacher that said he said the F-word, I knew my husband was going to point fingers. When "the word" slipped out, I had told Clayton it was a French word and he had to be eighteen to use it.

We are judged on our kids' actions and behaviors. This isn't always fair—some of the habits and actions that our children do are genetic, and I prefer to resort to blaming my husband's side of the gene pool for that!

When I asked my husband what age he started playing Little League baseball, he told me nine—that's probably why he was so much better than his son, who is only seven.

Before Children, I used to say those words: "Look at how good that child is, he must have good parents." I'm not going to rehash the nature versus nurture debate; it's more a "You get what you get" thing (see chapter 10). You can give them the tools, but they have to want to use them. Then again, maybe the apple doesn't fall far from the tree.

The Rule: *All you can do is all you can do.*

Get over yourself, and everybody else's expectations and opinions too. Take responsibility for the things you do have some control over, while you can, before they turn six and start fighting you every step of the way. Kids develop their own little minds and ideas about everything—someday, sooner than you are ready, they will be making their own decisions—so you've got to give them some experience making decisions and taking responsibility.

Rebel Rx:

1. "He's three." (Enough said.)
2. "She dressed herself today."
3. "His father made his lunch today." *(Note:* Blame Dad—he's always a good scapegoat.)
4. "I've been out of town. . . ."
5. "I don't know where he heard that word—must have been at the neighbor's."

PART THREE

The Perfect Family

Chapter 16

Like Cats and Dogs

The Myth: *Children raised in a common family environment have a natural bond.*

Which is more important—genetics or environment—in determining what a child will be like?

I don't know about that one, sorry. But it would seem to be a reasonable assumption that natural children of the same parents, raised in the same home, would have a lot in common. After all, if you follow the same cookie recipe, time after time, baked in the same oven . . . you should enjoy the same results, right?

And if that's true, then every trip to the same gene pool should result in children who would look alike in some ways. They should act alike and share similar views of the world. Of course, they wouldn't be twins or clones, but more alike than they are, say, with the family next door or down the street.

If all other factors remain constant, experience with Baby

#1 should prepare you for Baby #2. Baby #3 should be venturing further into familiar territory.

The Reality: *Cat-and-dog, night-and-day differences.*

I've heard it said the first child generally takes after the father, and the second child tends to favor the mother. In our house, that has proven to be true. Unfortunately, I never heard who the third child takes after. My husband wants to blame everything on the mailman, but our postal carrier is a big, black woman named Betty, and the results would be more obvious!

With my husband and me, it's always been a case of opposites attract, and maybe that explains it: how three children, with the same parents in the same home could be completely different: personalities, temperaments, even physical characteristics.

Aside from the obvious differences of boys and girls, somehow we've ended up with cats and dogs. Where did these kids come from?!

Baby #1, our older son, is just like his dad: long and lanky, laid-back and logical—fascinated by the way things work. He was an easy baby, always happy, healthy, generally agreeable, and highly social. He can't stand to be by himself. He will go anywhere on the weekend just to get out of the house. He is a very responsible child. He'll do anything for money. The neighbors love him and trust him to pet-sit when they are out of town. They encourage him to play with their younger kids because he's such a good role model.

We were completely unprepared for how different Baby #2, our only daughter, would be. She is her mother's daughter: hair, eyes, nose, and not a long or lanky bone in her body—she is a full-figured woman (solid, not chubby), like her Mom. She is the opposite of her brother in virtually every way: she is emotional, creative, strong-willed, temperamental, and not particularly social. She likes to be at home, happily plays by herself, drawing or coloring. When she does have a play date over, invariably it comes to: "Mrs. Caldwell, Haleigh isn't being nice. Will you play with me?" She is not motivated by money, and she prefers the scientific possibilities presented by younger kids and animals—for example: Will the rabbit fit in this box? Does the baby like orange soda?—to looking after them. She is not now, and probably never will be, in demand as a sitter for babies or pets.

And then we have Party Boy, Baby #3, our younger son. It's still early to come to any definite conclusions about this one, but he too will be his own person—and he's not having any of it from his older sister or brother. He likes to be involved, but unlike his brother, he's happy to play by himself. With an older brother and an older sister, he appreciates time when he can do what he wants, how he wants, without interference. Where his older brother tends toward moody, and his older sister can scream and pitch a fit to bring the house down, Tiger handles disagreement or disappointment very differently: He lays down on the floor and pretends to be dead (eyes closed, tongue sticking out). No drama, no kicking and screaming, no tears—just the lay-down. That's his way.

The Rule: *Celebrate unique personalities.*

Appreciate and foster your children's special strengths and talents. Each is individual. Resist the urge to compare.

Rebel Rx:

1. Wear identical neon T-shirts at crowded places like Disneyworld, so you'll be able to recognize each other and other people will know you belong together.
2. "Friends come and go, but you'll always have each other—so learn to get along." (Practice until you can shout it out from memory.)
3. Blame it all on the mailman!
4. Rebel Recommends: *Loving Each One Best: A Caring and Practical Approach to Raising Siblings* by Nancy Samalin and Catherine Whitney (Bantam Books).

Chapter 17

Civil War at Home

The Myth: *When the outside world is mean and cruel, they can always count on each other.*

The perfect family: two children, a boy and a girl, of course. The ideal timing between babies has never been determined, but wouldn't it be nice if they were a year or two apart—close enough to be friends. Best friends, they'll play together and keep each other company. They'll see each other at school, know all the same kids, and stick up for each other.

I didn't have much sibling experience when I was growing up. Since all seven of my half-brothers and half-sisters were eight-plus years older, and my parents divorced when I was very young, I essentially grew up as an only child, with *The Brady Bunch, Leave It to Beaver,* and *The Partridge Family* as my sibling role models. Brothers and sisters loved each other, helped each other, any and all problems were resolved by the end of the half-hour with goofy smiles and a group hug.

I thought my children would get along like that—the more, the merrier. Of course all kids quibble. People who live in close proximity to each other and have to share space and resources— kitchen privileges, a bathroom—will get on each other's nerves once in a while. My husband and I still quibble over who gets in the bathroom first—and how long it takes.

I would expect minor disagreements, lighthearted banter and teasing; even occasional knock-down, drag-out, high-decibel arguments—slamming doors—it happens. As long as they could hug and make up, apologize and get over it by the end of the day. At the bottom of it all, they would love and respect each other: Us against the world; blood is thicker than water.

The Reality: *They fight constantly, about everything.*

"He's touching me!"

"She's on my side!"

"I had that first!"

"Well, I was going to play with it . . ."

"It's *mine!*"

"That's *not fair!*"

"Mo-om!"

We have three wonderful children, boy-girl-boy, perfectly spaced by two and three years. The first to defend and protect each other? Not. On my daughter's first day of kindergarten, I was hesitant to let her ride the bus home, for fear her brother, an old pro in the second grade, would put her off the bus somewhere far from home. Not to worry—he simply refuses to acknowledge her at school; he'd blow his cover if he helped her get on or off the bus at any stop, right or wrong. "Zach has a sister?!" I get that all the time.

They fight about the color of the sky, who sits where in the car, who chooses . . . anything, whether it's what's for dinner or the program on TV, what game we're going to play, which pizza to order. Their favorite competition is who can speak loudest and longest to hold Mom's attention:

"Mom, guess what happened today . . . and then . . . and then . . . and then . . . blah blah blah . . . " Pretty soon, it stops making sense, whatever he's talking about—he just keeps on talking as fast as he can, without pause, louder and louder, while his sister winds up in the background: "Mommy! Mommy! Mommy . . . "

They provoke each other, put each other down. Their disagreements and conflicts are verbal and physical; but of course, he doesn't mean to trip her when he sticks his foot out every time she goes by. She retaliates by biting or scratching. Our day is a twenty-four-hour competitive marathon between Mr. Manipulator, The Drama Queen, and The Pawn (their little brother). With three children, I've hit my limit.

Blood is thicker than water? I haven't believed that since I found a Post-it note on the baby carrier: older brother offering his baby sister for sale for 50 cents. Carrier included.

My husband assures me they are completely normal—just like him and his brother when they were kids. And now he and his brother are best friends. "Well good for you!" I answer. "But how did your mother survive?"

The Rule: *Don't get caught in the middle.*

Sibling relationships are the first testing ground to learn negotiation and compromise. You don't need to know all the facts and arguments or take sides—be consistent, fair, impartial. Encourage them to work things out, but when it gets heated— divide and conquer.

Rebel Rx:

1. No weapons, for play or otherwise—they are inventive enough to come up with their own anyway.

2. Use odd/even or designated days of the week: Zach gets to choose first (whatever it is) on odd days, Haleigh gets even (days, that is). Fortunately, Tiger doesn't care yet, so it works for us now.

3. If they can't get along with each other, they can't play with friends—you have enough to deal with without OPMs.

4. If you are really feeling strong, lock them in a room together and force them to play games to learn how to share, take turns, win and lose graciously.

5. Rebel Recommends: *Siblings Without Rivalry: How to Help Your Children Live Together So You Can Live Too* by Adele Faber and Elaine Mazlish (Avon).

Chapter 18

Short-Order Cook

The Myth: *I'll decide what my children eat.*

Long before I had children of my own, I watched my neighbor one night, outside on her porch in the pouring rain, barbecuing a hot dog for her little princess, who was then about four years old. Nothing else was on the grill: She had an entirely different meal planned and prepared, which the Little Angel refused to eat. Hence, the emergency hot dog. In the rain.

I watched, and I listened to her daily dinner dilemma. I observed the crap she ate for lunch everyday with the child, and I vowed to myself and out loud: "I will never be a short-order cook!"

And, of course, I went on: "My children will eat the wonderful meals I lovingly prepare for them with smiles on their faces and gratitude in their hearts. They will exclaim "Ooh!" and "Ahh!," say "Please," and "Thank you!," and "Might I have some more, Mum?" (I'm not sure where that English accent came from, but that's how I imagined it!)

I envisioned their joy and delight over balanced, low-fat, sugar-free meals with fresh fruit and vegetables, never frozen, never from a drive-up window, enjoyed at the family dinner table with lively conversation and good manners. . . .

The Reality: *You have far less control than you think.*

We eat in two shifts: kids and then adults, usually after the kids are in bed. Have you ever tried a "family meal" around the table with three kids? "Ooh, aah, please, and thank you?" More likely "Yuck!," "Gross," and a nonstop, nerve-shattering battle for attention, who can talk the loudest and the longest, and who can make the biggest mess. The Little Angels are disgusting!

In preparing meals, I use all four burners on the cooktop, both ovens and the microwave, freezer selections and frequently the fast-food drive-up and/or pizza delivery service. I take full advantage of any and all resources, especially if it will save time.

And then there's the menu. We have the Picky Eater, who won't eat anything combined, sauced, or "touching" on the plate. He likes fresh vegetables (never cooked): carrots, cucumber slices, even green pepper—on the side. His favorite meal, after Chicken McNuggets and French Fries (with a toy!), is homemade pizza: mozzarella cheese on flatbread, no sauce; pepperoni, surprisingly, is permitted. Our daughter, bless her heart, will eat anything. And everything. As long as there is "dippin' sauce," ketchup preferred. And the youngest . . . well, he pretty much grazes all day long, helps himself to cheese and veggies during dinner prep, and is full by the time kid-dinner is on the table. But he'll eat anything with ketchup on it, anytime—thank goodness for the processed-tomato-and-sodium food group!

The Rule: *Compromise for peace and convenience.*

Never say never, especially out loud. Choose your battles with the kids, and make life easy on everyone: They will never appreciate Julia Child-type culinary creations, so keep it simple and healthy and let them choose—two options, max—and short-order it!

Rebel Rx:

1. Put Domino's and Pizza Hut on your speed-dial. Better yet, write the numbers, in permanent ink, on the inside of a kitchen cabinet or drawer (great place to keep the coupons too!).
2. Add shredded cheese. To anything. You can't go wrong with shredded cheese.
3. Don't fall for crazy colors (green ketchup, blue butter)—it's just *not worth it!* (Stains everything, besides being just plain gross.)
4. Teach your children to make good choices. Start the low-sugar lifestyle from the beginning (sugar really does make kids crazy—avoid it!), but don't make it a religion or an obsession.

Chapter 19

The Psychology of Money

The Myth: *My children will appreciate all that they have.*

When I was a kid, I knew the value of a dollar. I knew my mom, a single mother raising three kids on her own, worked very, very hard for her money. We didn't have a lot, but we had what we needed. We knew and appreciated that. We even had surprise extras every once in a while—but only once in a while. I knew to be grateful, happy with what I had, and not expect or ask for more. I knew it made my mom feel badly when I wanted something and we couldn't afford it.

In comparison, my children enjoy relative affluence in a very nice home with two parents who have a very comfortable income and lifestyle. As a new parent, I never thought much about kids in relation to money and financial education. I expected my children would understand and respect the value of the dollar too. Granted, that value is sadly diminished from the old days when a dollar would actually buy a snack, a drink, and a comic book with change left over.

The Reality: *Kids have no idea where money comes from and they don't care.*

One day, while grocery shopping with my sweet daughter, who was about four at the time, she wanted something of-the-moment in the store. Rather than just saying no, in the era of "use your words" and explaining and rationalizing everything to children ad nauseum, I said, "Mommy doesn't have the money for that today."

"Well, Mommy, just use your card."

"Sweetie, even when we use the credit card or the debit card, we still have to pay for it."

"Can you just get some money out of the wall?"

"What wall would that be?"

"The cash machine."

"The wall doesn't just give us money every time we ask for it."

"Yes it does." (Obviously, she's picked up her financial education from her father.)

"Honey, you know we have to put money into the bank in order to use our ATM card or get money out of the machine. We have to work very hard for that money."

I came to the sudden alarming conclusion that children rarely see that part of the transaction anymore. In the age of cashless transactions and automatic deposits, they never see the money going in! I went on in the misguided attempt to explain basic economic theory to a four-year-old in the check-out lane at the grocery store. Big mistake.

She rapidly fell back to more primitive methods, screaming her demands at the top of her lungs, jumping up and down and then falling to the floor, refusing to move until she got her whatever-it-was. But I've been there before, too. Embarrassing as it is, I refuse to give in, so I go primitive too—as calmly as possible. She can't hear anything I have to say anymore, but for the benefit of the check-out guy and everyone else in line, through gritted teeth, in the evil-Mommy voice I spit out, *"No, because I said so!"* I pick her up and carry her out of the store, kicking and screaming (her), smiling that "kids will be kids" smile (me), and assuring the bag boy, "Yes, I could definitely use some help out to the car, thank you!"

Economic theory and philosophy will have to wait for another, quieter, more rational time.

The Rule: *Just say No!*

Just because you can afford it, doesn't mean you should. The more you give, the more they expect. The desperately perceived value of any toy or impulse purchase ends as soon as it's home and out of the package. The further you let it get, the harder it is to ever go back, so just say *No!*

Rebel Rx:

1. Set up a chore chart; let them earn the things they want.
2. Make them "pay" Mom if she has to do their chores!
3. Use the Bank of Mom to credit and debit their account. Use a separate check register to keep track.
4. Don't give kids cash—they'll lose it and you'll end up finding it all over the house, suck it up in the vacuum cleaner, or wash and dry it in their pockets. (You get to keep whatever you find!)
5. Use toys to teach: Give them a play cash register with funny money; help them set up a little store or a pretend restaurant to learn and practice money.

Chapter 20

Too Much Time Together

The Myth: *Summer vacation and having quality time with the kids will be wonderful.*

Now that the kids are in school, I miss them! I find myself looking forward to summer break. We'll enjoy daily adventures and cultural outings to all the places we don't have time for during the school year: the park, the zoo, museums, and maybe even a family trip to Disneyworld.

Sometimes I worry, just a little bit, about all that time together, but I know we can do it—everyone else does! Everyone else is constantly telling me how much fun they have with their *great* kids. Take my friend Mary, for instance: She tells me about how she takes her children and all their friends to a different museum every week. She packs them lunch, transports them, and even swings by the library to get extra books on the subjects. They are keeping a journal to remember their cultural enrichment. She claims they are all "little angels" with such a thirst for knowledge.

And those Disney commercials . . . aren't they just everyone's fantasy? It makes my heart flutter to see the kids, parents, and even grandparents walking hand in hand, enjoying all the Disney amenities: the fairytale hotels, rides and attractions, pictures with Mickey, and dining with his character friends. It's no secret that I love roller coasters and have high hopes one of my kids will love the thrill as much as I do.

Summer will be terrific, and it will go by all too quickly. We are going to enjoy all the "extra" family time and then I am going to wish summer vacation was all year-round!

The Reality: *Having a lot of family time is overrated.*

"We're bored! We have nothing to do. . . . " Shoulders are slumped, and it's only the second day of summer break. I decide to brave it and take them to the new children's museum downtown. We finally get it together by noon, but are delayed by the words "I'm hungry!" for the tenth time. The short-order cook whips up another bowl of Rice Krispies, and we are off to gain some culture. I miss the exit off the interstate and have to endure my son saying:

"Mommy, are you lost again?"

"No Clayton, I am not lost, I just want to go a different way."

"Daddy says you always get lost."

"Well, Daddy isn't with us today, is he? He doesn't need to know!"

I locate the museum, only to find the parking garage is closed and parking is three blocks away in a garage lot built in the early part of the century. It is an SUV nightmare. I drive in reverse down three levels in order to let someone else out—this is scary, for I've been known to knock off a few mailboxes in my time. We make our way to the museum, and I spend $45 to let the kids play until they get bored. We leave after half an hour; so much for their thirst for knowledge.

I decide to brave the park. Lillian makes a beeline for the swings, jumps on, and does a splat (lets go while swinging in mid-air, without any attempt to get into a proper landing position) in the first five minutes, and we go home. That's enough culture and adventure for me for the entire summer, and it's only two o'clock! I decide to turn my attention and focus toward our Disneyworld family vacation and all the great fun we are going to have.

I spend eight hours packing the car. We planned to leave by 5:00 A.M., and finally are on our way at 9:00 A.M. As I turn around to catch Lillian getting carsick (no problem, I am prepared with bags . . . oops, the bag has a hole in it and I get it all over me), I hear Christmas music. "What is that?" It's a small Barbie Christmas tree Lillian snuck in the car; can't go to Disneyworld without a little Christmas in the summer! The eight-hour drive turns into thirteen hours of listening to "Santa Claus Is Coming to Town." We finally arrive at our Disneyworld paradise. The room looks a lot smaller than in the picture; we'll be really cozy in one bed. I call for dinner with Mickey—there is a six-month wait! Instead we order room service and eat cold limp hamburgers and retire to bed to the hum of a smelly air conditioner.

The next day we tour the Magic Kingdom. Lillian seems lethargic, and by the time we arrive at the front gate (which takes 45 minutes from our hotel), she's out cold. We spend our $250 to get in the gate, and she vomits and then passes out again. Clayton wants to ride the NASCARs (no takers for the rollercoaster), and the wait is three hours. Actually, the wait is three hours at every attraction. What do we do? We wait three hours for his three-minute thrill and decide to fight the crowd for some lunch. We search an hour for a hotdog, I send Clayton to scout out a table, and we finally settle in. As we bite into our cold dogs and greasy fries, Lillian wakes from her slumber and spills her cookies on the grandpa who's sitting at the table next to me. Fortunately, he has eight grandchildren and has seen it all before, so he is kind. I pay for his sandwich. Clayton's tired of waiting and wants to leave, but I am determined to get at least one picture with the famous rat. We loop around the park and there is no sign of him. No pictures with Mickey, no roller coaster—nothing. Time to go!

The next day, Brad and Clayton hang around the pool, where the decibel level is equal to an AC/DC concert—not at all quiet and peaceful like the commercials—while I sit in the room watching Lillian sleep. She never even naps at home, let alone sleeps for two days straight!

It's time to squeeze back in the car with the blinking, singing Barbie Christmas tree and drive home. When we arrive Lillian wakes up.

"Where is Mickey?"

"We're home already."

She starts to cry. "You promised me Mickey!"

The Rule: *Keep it simple.*

Quality time together is when everyone is having fun—including Mommy and Daddy!

Rebel Rx:

1. When you take them on the big trips, take *real* pictures—the screaming, crying, fighting, throwing up, sleeping—so you'll remember how it *really* was.

2. Cheap and easy alternative to Disneyworld: McDonald's Playland. Playtime and lunch for under $10, plastic souvenir included!

3. Summer camp—all-day summer camp—is a wonderful thing.

4. Tequila takes the edge off.

Chapter 21

Christmas & Other Blessed Events

The Myth: *The Norman Rockwell version of traditional Christmas.*

When I was a child, I loved the excitement of the holidays. At Christmas, I helped my mom wrap gifts and put up the tree. We baked cookies together, and I pored over the Sears catalog picking out my gift. It was simple and fun.

I envisioned my own family doing the same. Each night we'd sit down to watch a Christmas special, sipping our eggnog. We'd sing Christmas carols and bring yuletide cheer to everyone, creating family memories that the kids would cherish forever. The holiday spirit would permeate the air. I'd be like the good Martha Stewart and make thousands of homemade edibles with the children and send out a Christmas letter to keep all my friends up to date on our precious children and travels.

The Reality: *The season is total chaos.*

I have 365 days to plan until the big event, and somehow it sneaks up on me like an extra ten pounds. It's only Halloween, and I'm already tired of Christmas—I've been looking at Christmas stuff since July! Every New Year's Day I make a resolution: I will start my holiday shopping early enough to wrap all the gifts by September. Then I won't be a raving lunatic when December rolls around.

My husband would tell you I bring it on myself—why do I need two Christmas trees? Santa could spot our house from the moon with the amount of Christmas lights I put up. It's like I have a sickness—holiday-itis?—and I can't stop. I'm not the only one; my close friends all have it too. We make our daily runs to Michael's Crafts and Target to stock up on holiday supplies and, worse yet, crafts that require assembly! I get daily updates from Sherri: "Have you been to Target today? They have a nine-foot blow-up Santa that you have to have!" (Don't worry—she bought one for me.) The trouble with putting up so much is you have to take it all down and then pack it all away somewhere.

The weeks between Thanksgiving and Christmas become a blur. Between the holiday parties and the birthdays (everyone in my family has a December birthday; births in December should be outlawed) are the school parties. Every other day is an event, making ornaments, cards, cookies . . . and of course everyone needs a gift. . . . It goes on forever. I try not to get caught up in the mess, but still I find myself each year waking up in a cold sweat, worrying that I forgot to leave a gift for the mailman, or what about my hair dresser and the kids' piano teacher—what should

I get for them? I want to have a Christmas party this year, but who do I invite: neighbors, family, business associates, friends? How will I decide?

I tried baking cookies—once. I went out, bought all the ingredients and equipment: cookie cutters, sprinkles, decorations. I attempted to make the dough. Within the first five minutes, my daughter spilled all the decorations on the floor. The dog ate the dough when I bent down to clean the floor. I resorted to the slice and bake cookies, and told Aunt Jane it was hard work getting the little Christmas tree inside every circular cookie.

The whole Christmas card thing gives me hives. I have chucked the letter idea—too much work. Does everyone really need to know Uncle Harry is still in jail and my daughter tried to kill a bunny? I just wish people I don't know would stop sending me cards, so I don't feel obligated to send them one— who is my fourth cousin from Poughkeepsie, anyway?

The Rule: *Keep your expectations for the holidays in check.*

Stay out of the Christmas aisles at the store—the temptation to overdo it is just too great.

Rebel Rx:

1. Make your holiday To Do List early. Rip holiday To Do List in two. Throw one half away. Enjoy!

2. If Santa and everyone else is buying them toys, you don't have to!

3. Get Aunt Jane to bake cookies with the kids.

4. Send your Holiday greetings by e-mail—in January.

Chapter 22

Flying High

The Myth: *With good planning and preparation, you can enjoy long-distance travel with your children.*

Young children do not belong on airplanes. This is not a myth. Unfortunately, whether it's an emergency situation or overly optimistic vacation plans, sometimes you have to fly. Since it is illegal to leave children alone at home, and damn near impossible to find anyone willing to stay with your children overnight, sometimes it can't be helped—you find yourself flying high with kids.

"They'll be fine—we've brought all the snacks, blankies, and toys to keep them occupied. A ride on the airplane will be so exciting!"

Sure. All it takes is organization! When things get rough, you can always fall back on discipline and Rules:

1. There will be no getting sick on the airplane.
2. There will be no kicking the back of the seat in front of you.

3. There will be no yelling, screaming, or fighting.
4. There will be no leaving your seat!

"It's an adventure—and we are going to have *fun*, damn it!" If we run into any problems, I'm sure the flight attendants will come to our rescue. They are professionals; they handle situations like this all the time. The other passengers will be sympathetic to a little crying and noise; I'm sure they've all been through it themselves.

Having children will not cramp our travel plans. They'll have to adjust; what choice do they have?

The Reality: *Your children will make you and everyone else on the flight miserable.*

Emergency situation: a death in the family. We were living in Singapore and had not been back to the States in more than a year for two very good reasons: Clayton and Lillian, who were babies, only a year apart. (What were we thinking?)

I managed to finagle first class seating for four; we'd be fine. It's more schlepping than I had anticipated: two car seats, four carry-on bags, a double stroller, and let's not forget the kids! We get all snuggled in, with complementary cocktails for Mommy and Daddy, OJ for the kids. Everything is going well, no crying, no fussing—piece of cake! The flight takes off, and blast, boom, *Whaaaaaaaaaaaa!* It begins. Lillian starts with a primal scream that turns into a howl and then a constant growling cry. You don't know what that sounds like? It's not good. Imagine a dog caught in a leg trap for thirty-two hours. I still have scars from the daggers glared into my back from my twelve new friends in first class.

In desperation, I come up with an idea: We are in the very back row, in front of the engine, so I jam the screaming baby, in her car seat, behind our seats, hoping the noise will drown out the sound of her crying. Then I throw four blankets over her. While this is not recommended procedure—probably against FAA rules—it works! All is quiet. I start to worry, Am I smothering her? Can she breathe? Mommy panic takes over. I pick her up, bad idea: She turns into Mike Tyson and slugs me in the eye, ouch!

The glares, the whispers, the looks of the other passengers: "What's wrong with that child? What's wrong with that mother?" Okay, think . . . what to do? Clayton starts kicking the seat in front of him.

"Stop it, stop it Clayton! I mean it!"

Finally, we land in Tokyo. Six hours into the trip from hell, we question ourselves, Should we turn around? The doors open. The minute we are off the plane, Lillian stops crying and Clayton stops kicking. Our layover is filled with the usual: spilled juice, diaper changing, me crawling on the bathroom floor looking for Clayton's favorite toy. We press on. Back to the plane we go. Our "friends" are waiting for us.

I'm tired, grumpy, embarrassed and, of course, the minute we are on the plane Lillian starts in. A flight attendant approaches. I'm sure she's about to ask me to parachute off the plane with my screaming child. No, wait. She looks sympathetic; she must be a mother. She brings an entire bottle of wine and sets it in front of me.

"Honey, you need this. Drink up."

I comply. I'm sleepy and couldn't care less that Lillian is still crying. My husband, fresh from a dead-to-the-world nap, offers to take over. He and Hellion disappear into the loo so she can play with the tampons and sanitary napkins for the next four hours (apparently this is great entertainment for her). Turbulence brings them back to their seats. The minute she's back in her seat the wailing begins again. I stuff her behind the seat again; the flight attendant pretends not to notice. Six hours straight, Lillian goes and goes and goes until we hear the wonderful announcement: "Ready for landing."

I try to get myself together, wipe the mascara from under my eyes, comb the rat's nest hair, spray some perfume to cover the vomit—Lillian vomits when she gets upset. Only on me, though. Our seats look like a fraternity house after a party; we make an effort to clean up. Waiting for the doors to open, the plane is so quiet you could hear a pin drop. Did I mention that both kids have fallen fast asleep in the last five minutes? To break the silence I shout out: "Well, now you know why I use birth control!" Small chuckle; really small chuckle. We descend off the plane with our two sleeping angels and everything else, less the stuff we've lost or abandoned. We are already dreading the return trip—by boat, might be easier!

The Rule: *Plan your travel with realistic expectations.*

What can you do? Grin and bear it? It will be a challenge. When you are traveling and see another parent struggling with her children, be kind. Try a smile or offer to help, so she at least gets a bathroom break by herself. It can make all the difference.

Rebel Rx:

1. Drive. It's a lot easier than flying, and you can yell at them in private.
2. Dress everyone in black. Even if you are not flying to a funeral, if everyone thinks you are flying with these horrid children because you *have* to, you'll get sympathy points.
3. Always buy the headphones—give them out to the people around you. Apologize ahead of time.
4. Never take a child on a flight longer in hours than his age in years.

PART FOUR

Life in the Village

Chapter 23

Empty Nesters

The Myth: *The grandparents will always be available to baby-sit and will never interfere or offer unsolicited advice.*

The empty nesters (prospective grandparents) have been talking about me having children since the day I was married:

"You don't want to be too old when you have kids—you need to think about having them soon."

"You look pregnant—are you? Why not?!"

"I can't wait to baby-sit."

"When you have children, we'll be there to help every step of the way."

With such wonderful support—my own little village to sustain me—I was not concerned about having children. My village consists of my immediate family. My parents and in-laws are the head Kahunas. When our small village is together, they pow-wow about the prospect of being grandparents. They dwell on what the kids will look like: Will they have Aunt

Jane's blonde hair, Grandpa's height, or Grandma's Pacific-blue eyes? I can hear them already ooohing and aaahing over my wee ones. They won't be able to get enough of them.

The Reality: *Empty nesters think they want to spend lots of time with their grandchildren, until they actually do.*

"Could you ask your parents to baby-sit on Friday?"

"I did, they're busy playing tennis. Ask your parents."

"I did—they said Dad's back hurts and Mom has a cold."

"They always have an excuse! 'I'm tired, we have a Grand Poo-Ba meeting, we have no plumbing, the car doesn't have gas. . . . ' It's always something!"

"When is the last time they baby-sat?"

"When we just had one. . . . "

The first grandchild gets it all. Everyone fights over who gets to watch him, he's showered with gifts, and no one forgets his birthday. Then along comes the second; more diapers to change, someone for the first one to fight with, double the work, and poof—just like magic everyone in the village disappears.

They discuss who looks like whom, and if they don't like what they see, they blame the other gene pool:

"We never had a nose like that in our family."

"You kids had hair as babies."

They seem to enjoy the idea of grandparenting much more than the reality. They go to bed at night whispering to each other, or worse, sharing with you less-than-subtle comments:

"Our kids never did that. They had manners."

"We disciplined our children!"

"You should . . ."

"Why don't you . . ."

You will hear how their kids slept through the night at six weeks, were potty trained at two, and *never*, under any circumstance, slept in their parents' bed.

When Clayton was six weeks old, I brought him to my parent's home for a viewing—a party my mother had to show him off. One of the empty nesters asked me where Clayton slept; I nonchalantly told her with me. This caused her to let out a shriek and drop her coffee. All the other empty nesters at the gathering came running to see what was wrong. I'll never forget what she said: "You've ruined him—ruined him!" She was shaking as she said it. I ran to my bedroom and cried the rest of the day. What had I done? Did I cause permanent damage?

I went home the next day, waited until nightfall, and put him in his crib. I hovered over him, waiting to see how I had ruined him. Maybe he'll never be able to sleep alone. Maybe he'll think sleeping is always a threesome! In two minutes, he was in Dreamland, and he slept all through he night (he did that in my bed, too). That was the moment I realized not everything the old birds tell you is true.

The empty nesters have selective amnesia about the children they raised, but I think that's the brain's way of preserving the happy memories. I even catch myself some days, watching my friends with children younger than mine and thinking, "My children never did that!"

The Rule: *Remember the dubious value of experience in hindsight.*

Don't be a rocking chair quarterback when you are an empty nester!

Rebel Rx:

1. Be careful waiting too long to have kids—the older you are, the older Grandma and Grandpa are, and they will be even less willing and able to help.
2. Find a great baby-sitter so you don't always have to rely on Grandma.
3. Ignore any comments and suggestions that begin with: "You need to . . . You should . . . Why don't you . . . "
4. Nod and smile. They mean well—I think.

Chapter 24

The Social Life of Moms

The Myth: *The International Motherhood Club—you'll always have someone to talk to.*

It's true that everything changes, especially after the Big Events in your life—graduations, marriage, babies. Naturally, these events lead to new interests, new people, new issues and concerns—a New You.

But even though everything changes, you would think, as a mom, it would be easy to make and keep new friends. After all, you have the universal language of motherhood, which bonds you to all women who have been through the birth experience. You may be a world apart in culture and location, but with kids—you have something in common with all mothers everywhere. In your own community and neighborhood, there are so many opportunities for friendship: children's activities, parks, church, and school—the PTA is nothing but a gang of new friends just waiting for you!

The New Me walked out of my office for the last time two weeks before my first child was due. I had no intention of going back to work after my six weeks' maternity leave—or ever. I kept in touch for a short time with my coworkers and job-related friends—enough to visit and show off that beautiful baby—but very quickly, we had very little in common. While I was home all day in my PJs dealing with breastfeeding, bathing, and burping a baby, in a semi-comatose but blissfully happy state of round-the-clock baby love and sleep deprivation . . . they all still got up every morning, got dressed, and rushed to get to the office on time to do . . . well, pretty much the same things I had done every day, day in and day out, for all those working years. I'd been there, done that, so none of the office gossip was all that interesting compared to my new baby and all the fascinating things happening to me at home . . . but my former colleagues didn't seem to be interested. They'd eagerly hold the baby for a minute and coo and babble a bit, but then they were done. And the conversation was pretty much over.

I wasn't worried though: I had new friends. The last couple of months of my pregnancy, I had snuck out on my lunch hour to a prenatal yoga class and met a group of women who were just like me (hugely pregnant). I had a dozen new best friends, all of whom would have babies about the same time. I had coffee dates, lunch buddies, and, best of all, play group! Our New Mommies Club got together faithfully once a week, in each other's homes, before and after all the babies came, and it was wonderful—we all had so much in common! We bonded through the birth and early infancy experience. I was happy. I looked forward to being with these women, growing with them and their children, for the next eighteen years and beyond.

The Reality: *If it's so easy to make and keep new friends, why do I feel so alone?*

The yoga play group was wonderful, so easy at first when we all had brand-new babies. Everything was new and exciting. We all had so much to talk about, comparing notes and sharing advice. And we were all so sleep deprived and so deeply in New Mommy shock, it was quite a while before any of us realized we really only had one thing in common. We were drawn together by conceptual timing—coincidence—and not much else.

Strange things started happening within our little group: We tried to get the husbands involved in family play dates. The men didn't have anything in common, mostly because they were all different ages, mid-twenties to nearly sixty. Yes, they all had new babies, but the men didn't bond as easily over birth stories and developmental issues.

This highlights a cold, hard reality: The Family Compatibility Factor. It is nearly impossible to find another mother you like and could be friends with, and have the whole family package mix well. If you like the mother, will you like the husband too? Can you stand the kids, and does your husband like everyone, too—and vice versa? The more elements to the equation (number and varying ages of children), the more difficult it is to find a "match."

The second challenge in the yoga play group was physical proximity. Although we all started off in town, many of the new families moved out to the suburbs to bigger houses and better schools. We started driving farther and farther for our weekly get-togethers, which became more and more of a challenge with a screaming baby in the car seat during those long drives. As the children got older and more individual, all the differences among our group became more apparent, from parenting ages and issues, to discipline, marriage philosophies, back-to-work or stay-at-home decisions, religion, and education.

By the time the second wave of babies came around, the group had disbanded. I was on my own with two young children. These became my early Internet years, when I found solace and companionship in e-mail correspondence and online interaction with women like myself all over the world—it was easier to e-mail and get to know another mom online during the peace and quiet of naptime. I had neighborhood friends, too, but it was difficult to get together with kids on different nap and activity schedules. When we did get together, we never actually got to engage in meaningful conversation or even talk in complete sentences while we were chasing toddlers.

Then school started. Somehow, just when I thought friends would be easier to find, it was just the opposite. Sure, there were a lot of moms, and plenty of opportunity to socialize and get involved, but the difficulty of The Family Compatibility Factor was the same—invariably, we'd like the kids and hate the parents, or love the parents and not be able to tolerate their little monsters! And the whole PTA thing . . . well, to be perfectly honest, the PTA serves a noble and valuable function in the school community, but it's also a hotbed of political intrigue and gossip, where conformity is your best bet.

The problem is, I never could stand to be just like everybody else. Rebel Housewives can be a solitary bunch—let's face it, we are pretty unique, good or bad, depending upon your perspective. With kids, you have less time in general and no time to waste. You have to really like someone to want to give up your oh-so-valuable kid-free time to hang out. There are Rebel Housewives all around, but they are just as busy as you are.

I was in a new neighborhood, just after the birth of my third child; the two older ones were in school five days a week. The Family Compatibility Factor had kicked in, and there was already a turf battle in the neighborhood between the crazy woman with the nice kids next door and the great mom with possessed devil-children across the street. The best tactic was simply to withdraw. Just when I finally decided I was a loner, and happy to be that way—along came Vicki.

The Caldwells and The Roos proved to be a unique and powerful combination, a perfect match on The Family Compatibility Scale:

- We lived down the street from each other, which is probably better than right next door, as you don't want to be too close and know too much.
- The kids were the same age and sex; they all got along

great with each other and were nice and respectful to all the parents—not OPMs (see chapter 25).

◦ The husbands got along well, when they saw each other, and we were able to enjoy time together as families and as adults away from the kids, too.

◦ Among the mix of parents and kids, we had strong, yet complementary personalities. We had four laid-back, easy-to-get-along-with boys (including the husbands), four girls (including me and Vicki) bitchy enough to stand up to each other and get along, and the baby, Tiger Scott, who was everyone's darling.

The only problem is, over four terrific years of friendship, our families became quite interdependent and exclusive—it was just easier to hang out together than branch out. Then our best friends and my Rebel Partner moved to Hong Kong on a job transfer—we were on our own again!

Thank goodness for the Internet—it's nice to be right down the street, but the Internet makes it possible to be halfway around the world and still carry on a Rebel Friendship.

The Rule: *Use a careful selection strategy.*

Quality of friendship, rather than quantity of acquaintances and commitments, is what matters most. Search for the other Mom who is just a little different from the rest—you will recognize her, as it takes one to know one.

Rebel Rx:

The Tests of Rebel Friendship:

1. You have contact every day—by e-mail, phone, even face to face.

2. You list each other as emergency contacts and alternate phone numbers.

3. You can tell each other everything—even the worst things you could never tell anyone else—and it doesn't go any farther.

4. She'll drop everything and take your kids as her own in an emergency.

5. She's your Go-to Girl in a crisis, whether it's someone to listen, reassure, advise—or just be at your house for the repairman.

6. You can trust her to talk to your kids—she'll tell them what you want to say, and then she'll tell you what they say. The kids never need to know. They'll listen to her.

7. She's the person your kids plan to run away to when you are just too awful. (My kids are going to have a challenge to get all the way to Hong Kong now, instead of just down the street!)

Chapter 25

OPMs (Other People's Monsters)

The Myth: *The Kool-Aid Mom, as seen on TV.*

Women who become mothers, especially stay-at-home moms, love all children. They have a natural instinct, the compulsive need and desire to nurture anyone and everyone under the age of eighteen. They speak the language. They cuddle and coo over babies. They are always available and happy to baby-sit, carpool, play date, and volunteer for all school-related activities and community service. They aspire to be The Kool-Aid Mom, serving refreshments and a smile to all the neighborhood kids in their yard every day.

When I was younger, before I had children and neighborhood kids of my own and still thought all kids were adorable—I wanted to be that mom. The cool mom, the one everyone likes. I would watch over all of them, my children and all of their buddies. I'd have refreshments, I'd always welcome an extra kid or two at the dinner table. We would have sleepovers! I would encourage them to play at our house. It was the perfect plot to know where and what my kids were doing and who they were hanging out with.

The Reality: *Having kids doesn't make you Mother Teresa.*

I love my children and delight in their company. Other people's monsters? Not so much. Babies really don't turn me on. Been there, done that. As for The Kool-Aid Mom, well . . . do you know how much sugar is in that stuff? Do you really want a gang of sugar-hyped kids running screaming around your house? Somebody falls down, gets hurt—these days, even neighbors will sue!

I tried to be The Gatorade Mom for a while, but ended up frustrated and angry when they all left their drink boxes and garbage all over the house and yard. They ate and drank me out of house and home. And all the mess and noise! I spent hours cleaning up what took them ten minutes or less to trash.

Parents come in all shapes and sizes and along with that comes all different rules. Unfortunately, we can't hand-pick our neighbors, and we are forced to live with the kids that come along with the neighborhood:

The kid who never has to go home.

The kid who is always hungry when he comes over.

The kid who has no rules or discipline at home.

The kid who has no manners.

The kid who teaches the others all the swear words he learns from his parents.

I have a low tolerance for chaos. My kids are aware of this, and we manage fairly well as a family. In the neighborhood, I'm known as the mom who goes crazy if they all don't pick up after themselves. Mommy Dearest makes them eat their treats in the kitchen and won't let them watch TV. The kids who come a-calling don't mess with "The General," as I'm referred to; however, there are times when it's beyond my control.

Our first sleepover occurred because we were helping friends who had to go out of town for a family emergency. It was a school night and I was trying to get the kids to bed early. Our little guest refused to go to sleep, even with my threat that I would tell Santa. He proclaimed he never bathed and didn't have to go to bed before midnight. After a long struggle, he was finally asleep at 11:30 P.M. , only to be wandering the house again by 3:00 A.M. He was looking for ice cream—we didn't give him dessert! (Because he didn't eat his dinner.) He was so loud, everyone woke up, and next thing I knew we were all eating bowls of vanilla ice cream in the wee hours. The next day was miserable, with grumpy, sleepy, over-sugared kids. That was the end of the sleepovers.

I started to be more and more reclusive, getting my kids more involved in after-school activities and not answering the phone or the door if the visitor was under eighteen without an accompanying adult.

It's bad enough, even when you can trust your own children to be good, to know and follow the basic rules of proper social interaction and respect—you can't be sure OPMs have been brought up to the same standards.

The Rule: *Establish minimum entrance requirements for visiting kids.*

These include respect, "Please," "Thank you," flushing the toilet, picking up after yourself, and throwing your trash in a garbage can (which should not, incidentally, be used for any other purpose, including science experiments, basketball, dunking tanks, holders of small children, or kick the can).

When the fangs and claws start to show—send them home! And no: You don't have to let them back in. Ever.

Rebel Rx:

1. Establish rules and consequences (You'll go home!) up front—popularity is overrated.
2. If you make OPMs follow the rules at your house, they won't want to come back anyway.
3. Kids should eat at their own house.
4. Make a schedule with the other neighborhood moms: Let them all play until 5:00 P.M., and then everyone should go home for dinner, homework, cleanup, bedtime.
5. When it's time to go home, give everyone the 15-minute warning—set the egg timer!—for cleanup and clear-out.

Chapter 26

It's a Strange, Strange World

The Myth: *The world was a much safer place when we were growing up.*

"When I was your age . . . " You're rolling your eyes already, aren't you? Just like you did whenever your parents started off that way—maybe you still do. Fortunately, we don't have to walk five miles to school . . . both ways . . . uphill . . . in the snow. Our lives are very different now. The world has changed, and it continues to change at a mind-boggling pace. Do you ever find yourself going into that routine with your children? "When I was a kid . . . "

   We listened to records on a turntable, and then we had eight-track tapes! We had to get up to change the channel on TV, and we had to watch our favorite programs when they were scheduled—with commercials. We had to write or type papers and reports on a machine called a typewriter—there used to be typewriters in every office instead of computers. When we wanted to communicate with friends or family, we wrote letters or picked up the phone to call—from home, since we didn't have cell phones. We had to sit down when we used the phone; our roaming range was limited by the length of the cord. We listened to the radio in the car (FM was a big step forward), and had to go to the theatre to see movies. A calculator was about as high tech as it got.

But, as hard as it was in the "dark ages," without all the wonderful benefits of technology we enjoy today, we were safe. Life was simple; we enjoyed a lot of freedom; we rode our bicycles without helmets; teachers, police officers, and adults in general were safe. At least with the benefit of hindsight through a hazy nostalgic lens, childhood was an idyllic time.

The Reality: *The world is a dangerous place today, but it was dangerous when we were kids too.*

Is it really that the world has changed so much, or is it us? Being the mom, we can't help but see everything from a different perspective. Everything seems so dangerous, and every adult is suspect. It seems we are teaching kids, earlier and earlier, things we never knew about and had to figure out on our own: drugs, sex, AIDS, politics.

I don't remember this structured concept of "play dates" when I was a kid: We roamed the neighborhood and played with whomever we found. The neighborhood was anywhere we could walk to or get to on our bikes—we rode our bikes on the street, through intersections and everything! We'd be gone for hours at a time.

Last year, my son reached the age of greater independence: eight years old. He wanted to go, go, go. I tried to be encouraging; I tried to give him more freedom, but it was a difficult transition. We don't live in a small town; we live off of a very busy street in a big city, with lots of cars, lots of strangers, danger everywhere. I have to know where he's going, who he's hanging out with, when he'll be back. He is a great kid. We've taught him well, and I trust him to make good decisions; but still—every minute he's gone, I imagine the worst and worry about cars, strangers, dogs, older kids, poison ivy, and snakes. It is tough to be Mom!

It doesn't help to think about all the crazy, stupid things we did as kids—the least of which was riding our bicycles without helmets—and wonder how we ever survived. How did our mothers cope? Wait a minute—they never knew half of the trouble we got into . . . but my kids wouldn't do any of that stuff, would they?

The Rule: *Be vigilant with your kids, but be reasonable.*

Teach your children well and protect them, but be willing to let go, a little bit at a time. Let them take small steps toward independence and making their own decisions—you can't always be there, Mom.

Rebel Rx:

1. Define your neighborhood, and your rules, and make sure your kids know the boundaries.
2. Enlist your neighbors. It helps to have eyes and ears up and down the street.
3. Strap a walkie-talkie to your kid so you can call him and he can call you.
4. Have the kids play in groups; there is always a tattletale or informant.
5. Listen and talk with your kids. Discuss issues and events, so they have a better understanding of the world and the vocabulary to tell you anything.

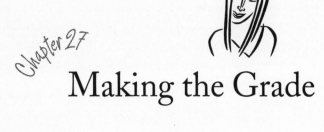

Chapter 27

Making the Grade

The Myth: *Public school was good enough for me and will be for my kids, too.*

My children's education will fall into place. School will take care of itself, just like when I was a kid. My mother simply signed us up at the local public school and off we went—yes, on foot. There was nothing else to it—and look how great I turned out! She didn't spend any time checking my homework in elementary school, because I didn't have any.

My mom never lost any sleep wondering if I was going to get into college—if I didn't, I'd have to figure it out. Mothers today stress out about this "school thing." They have fallen into the trap of creating Superkids. They bombard their poor children with flash cards, tutoring, workbooks, and lessons for everything, all before they go to kindergarten. They put their kids on a wait list for preschool! Not me—I'm going to let my kids be kids. What's the rush?

The Reality: *Three decades later, even preschool is competitive.*

It begins while you are pregnant, the bombardment of information on how to make your child smart: play classical music, eat certain foods. . . . The list goes on, and the pressure builds. With each month after birth, everything is measured. How many words does he say? Can he read and tell time? Does he know his capitals? The question "Where is your son going to go to school?" is always followed by a condescending "Oh," and noses turn up. How did it come to this?

I started losing sleep, wondering if my son would be able to make the grade. We started applying for exclusive preschools.

I carefully prepared my son for his first interview. He was three. I went over the strategy for weeks: Be polite and sit still. I promised him a new Matchbox car if he was a "good boy."

The morning of the big day I knew I was in trouble. He was tired and whiney. We got to the school, and there were about 500 people applying for three openings. I had heard legendary rumors about the rigorous process of getting into a private school; now I was living it. During the three-hour screening process the school tests the kids, interviews them, and observes them.

A teacher emerged and took Clayton away for his individual, then group, interviews. The parents were asked to wait behind. I crossed my fingers and prayed he wouldn't use any poopy words. Brad and I waited for the next three hours, pacing the corridors with the other parents, making small talk about how smart our kids are and how much we *love* the school. After what seemed like an eternity, we were invited to retrieve our children and join the last five minutes of observation. I sighed with relief: We were almost through the process, unscathed. Even if we don't get in this year, we still might have a chance next year.

I beamed proudly as I saw Clayton sitting quietly, behaving nicely, no picking his nose or loud outbursts. As we were about to exit the classroom, I paused to greet and thank the teacher, hoping she would remember me and my son kindly. As I was shaking her hand, Clayton went over to the hamster cage and spit—yes, spit!—into the cage. The teacher gasped and grabbed her heart.

"Clayton, what are you doing?"

"Don't like it, Mom."

"Clayton, apologize!"

"No."

"Yes!"

"No!"

I felt the blood drain from my face, and I profusely offered my apologies to the teacher. I swear I saw her go and cross his name off the list! I grabbed Clayton and carried him out in the fireman's hold—you know, when you put you arm around their waist, head facing forward, legs dangling, and run.

I saw Harvard slipping away and vocational school in our future. When we got home, I asked my son why he spit on the hamster.

"Mom, it was there."

I gave up and thought to myself, "My god, he is only three, what do I expect?" Why do I feel so much pressure for him to succeed? I know why—it's all around me. The neighbor kid already knows the violin, takes French lessons, and plays the piano—he's only five. I feel like I'm not doing my job—my kids only have one activity and go to bed by seven! Push, push, push—this is what parents do.

The Rule: *Don't get obsessed with creating the perfect child.*

Learning is supposed to be fun, not a job. Kids are supposed to be kids, not miserable little adults.

Rebel Rx:

1. As my mother says, "Don't worry, they all learn to read eventually!"
2. There is just something wrong when a five-year-old is smarter than you are.
3. Don't compare your kids with the neighbors. Do you really want your kids to be like OPMs?

Mental Health Days

Chapter 28

The Myth: *Sick days are only for when you are sick.*

Rules are meant to be followed. Schedules are in place for everyone's benefit. The world will stop and spin out of control if you are off one day from school or work. . . .

"If you miss more than ten days of school, excused or not, they'll send 'd-fax' to your door. They are very serious about attendance policy."

This from our neighbor, Karen, just before our oldest child started kindergarten in the public elementary school. She was concerned because we had been talking about our annual cruise for Zach's birthday in January. (Back in the day when we had money to go on a cruise every year.)

Hmmm. This could be a problem for us. Before we had children, and when the kids were young, we got in the habit of off-season travel, mostly because that's when we could get time off. While everybody else went during school vacations, we lived life opposite the school schedule, cruising the

Caribbean in January and vacationing in the mountains, at the beach, and at Disneyworld while school was in session. We learned to love the off-season crowds—the lack of them, especially OPMs—and the off-season rates.

"What the heck is a 'd-fax' anyway?"

Actually, that's DFACS: Department of Family and Child Services. Atlanta Public Schools takes their strict attendance policy *very* seriously. (It must have something to do with government statistics and funding appropriations, although they don't admit that.)

The Reality: *Mental Health Days can keep you from getting sick, plus you get a whole lot more enjoyment out of a Sick Day when you are not physically sick.*

Actually, they don't send DFACS—they send letters and warnings. We failed attendance the first year, and we didn't even get to the Caribbean in January! No, that was the year Zach's annual fall allergies kicked in, and he missed several days in the first month of school.

Kindergarten was also the year Grandpa Caldwell went into the hospital after a stroke, and we rushed the family up to St. Louis to spend a week with him and the rest of the family, afraid it might be our last chance. As it turned out, it was. Grandpa Caldwell passed away in February, and we were back in St. Louis for the funeral. These were the events around which a rigid attendance policy, especially in kindergarten, just didn't matter. Let them send DFACS. (If we had not gone to St. Louis, we would have gone on the cruise!)

Aside from legitimate absences, I've long been a proponent of Mental Health Days and The Joy of Hookey, within reason. I corrupted my husband with this philosophy when we were in college. It was almost twenty years ago, but I clearly remember the Mondays we were headed back to school for the week . . . and just kept going. We spent one gorgeous day of hookey at the top of Mt. Rainier outside of Tacoma, Washington. Another day we spent on the Washington State Ferry, day-tripping through the San Juan Islands. It was magical. I could not recall for you one individual day of school with any clarity, but I can remember every detail of those Mental Health Days. And the world did not fall apart in our absence. No one even noticed.

The Rule: *Indulge in a Mental Health Day.*

Every once in a while, when you don't have a crisis to handle or an important appointment, do it. It's okay. I'll write you a note.

Rebel Rx:

1. Go to an afternoon movie during the week while everybody else is working.
2. Take the time to write very creative excuse notes for school or work—your boss or teacher will really appreciate it!
3. The age-old, irrefutable, can't-be-rejected, very best excuse to give for a Mental Health Day (even if it's

not true): PMS or "girl trouble." (Might as well enjoy one benefit from the monthly curse.)

4. Rebel Recommends: *Celebrate Today: Over 3000 Boss-Proof, Tamper-Resistant, Undeniable Reasons to Take the Day Off* by John Kremer (Open Horizons).

PART FIVE

Men, Sex, & Other Fantasies

Chapter 29

Sex, Lies, & Videotape

The Myth: *Married people have sex all the time.*

Sex, sex, sex—it's all-pervasive. From the constant bombardment of sex in the media—magazines, music, movies, advertising, television (especially that nympho Samantha on *Sex in the City)*—you'd think everybody is doing *it,* all the time. It's going on all around us: at home, at the office, in dressing rooms, restaurant bathrooms, airplanes!

How does all of this sex affect marriage? Ideally, of course it is husbands and wives, married to each other, and other committed couples having a good share of the fun. We know there is a lot of other stuff going on, but let's look at sexpectations in marriage: What is really going on in everybody else's marital bedroom? Are married people enjoying sex all the time? As much as they hoped? As much as they claim?

Men and women come into marriage with similar expectations. Men assume that marriage allows for unlimited sex-on-demand—it was in the vows somewhere, wasn't it? Newlywed brides, too, look forward to indulging—finally guilt-free!

In the early days, the honeymoon continues and it is wonderful! The only problem with all that great sex becomes apparent sooner or later: pregnancy. Oops or not, a baby changes everything . . . .

The Reality: *Having kids is stressful on the sex life.*

"Want to have sex tonight?"

"I don't know."

"What kind of an answer is that?"

"I'm just sooooo tired. . . ." After the baby, those four words will be the major sex block for the next twenty years. "Clayton was up all night last night, he didn't nap all day, I can't remember when I showered last—and I think I'm getting PMS."

"Wow, that puts me in the mood."

We both roll over and go to sleep—again. It has been a week or more since we've made love. In the morning, after another sleep-interrupted night of crying, feeding, and changing the baby (remember when it was multiple orgasms in one night instead of multiple feedings and poopstorms?), hubby tries again.

"Not even! Go away—don't you have to get to work?"

He's sweet—and persistent: "Let's do it this afternoon during the nap. I'll pop home from work for a quickie!"

"Okay, later. Love you. Bye." A few more precious minutes of sleep before it all starts again with the crying and the feeding and the pooping. . . .

But I make an effort. I roll out of bed and manage a quick shower before the first call to duty. By 11:00 A.M. , I'm getting kind of excited: We are going to have sex! Naptime rolls around; I put Clayton in bed. He immediately begins screaming, "No nap! No nap!" I spend the next hour wrestling with him to lie down. By now, hubby has been home half an hour and I'm a little disheveled, but not discouraged, still feeling amorous. Okay, horny.

"Vik, I've got to get back to work!"

"I know—I'm trying. . . ."

I sneak out of Clayton's bedroom. "Let's turn on the music so we can't hear him cry." I crank the volume. With no time to change the CD, we begin trying to have crazy, passionate, spontaneous sex (as scheduled) to "Winnie the Pooh Playtime." In the interest of time, with only fifteen minutes left before he has to get back to a meeting, we whip off our clothes and get right to business. I close my eyes to conjure up some romance.

"Brad, that tickles! . . . Ohhhh, Brad, that really tickles!"

"What are you talking about?"

I open my eyes: Clayton! "What are you doing out of your crib?"

"Mama, mama bird, mama naked!" He's holding a feather and tickling my behind! I dash for my clothes and quickly cover everything.

"Mommy and Daddy are just doing laundry, Honey!" So much for being in the mood. Try again later? Off Brad goes, back to work, disappointed, frustrated, without a trace of the much-anticipated afterglow of a man who just got laid.

Determined to make it work, I plan a romantic dinner and tell him to be home by 5:00 P.M. (If it's any later than that, I'm afraid I'll be too tired.) I light the candles, set the table, put on makeup, and get Clayton in front of the VCR to watch *The Lion King*. No surprises this time; let Disney entertain him while we have sex! Brad enters the house and I'm at the dining room table waiting for him (no music this time, just the gentle murmur of Elton John singing "Circle of Life"). In the interest of time, eighty-eight run-time minutes and counting, I'm already naked.

"Wow, I can't wait to eat!" He strips down and we begin eating, sipping wine, talking dirty. . . . It's going great, all is quiet with Clayton and *The Lion King*—forty-four minutes left! The doorbell rings. My mother-in-law is standing on the front porch! Can't she ever call first?

"Oh—hi, Mom! We were just, uh, doing laundry. . . . "

The Rule: *Where there's a will and a VCR, there's a way!*

Keep trying—don't ever give up! Enjoy what works for you, and don't worry about what everybody else is doing. (As far as having *it* daily—they are lying!)

Rebel Rx:

1. Lock your bedroom door.
2. Enjoy great sex during the day when the kids are at school!

3. Take the kids over to Grandma's or to the baby-sitter's house, and go back home instead of going out.

4. Learn to appreciate the art of the quickie!

5. Oysters and wine make great aphrodisiacs; hot peppers make everything more spicy!

6. Rebel Recommends: *How to Cook For Your Man & Still Want to Look at Him NAKED* by Lori and Vicki Todd (Oxmoor House).

Chapter 30

Who Said Bigger Is Better?

The Myth: *A bigger, more expensive house guarantees a better life.*

Several years ago, during the heyday of the technology wonder years, my husband and I, for one brief time in our lives, were rich, rich, rich! On paper, anyway. The software company he had built from two guys in our basement to more than 300 employees in offices all over the world was about to Go Public, which meant all that paper wealth would soon be cash money, and we would be set for life—several lifetimes. We started looking at real estate—movin' on up, just like the Jeffersons.

In 1994, we had scraped to buy our first cozy, little home in Atlanta: a 1950s brick ranch in a quiet cul-de-sac neighborhood "inside the Perimeter" (the I-285 interstate that encircles metro Atlanta), but far from the fancy upscale environs of Buckhead or Morningside. We paid $90,000 for 2,000 square feet: two bedrooms, one and a half bathrooms, a half-finished daylight basement, an open one-car carport, and a big backyard for Shaney and Data, our two-year-old mutts. It was perfect.

We were very happy in our little house for six years. We had two children, who shared one small bedroom, and wonderful neighbors, whom we enjoyed seeing and visiting with all the time, especially Friday nights (Margarita Night!) on the driveway or in one of our front yards.

Russ started the business in 1996. By the end of 1999, three short years later, we were looking at million-dollar properties in ultra-trendy Buckhead. Bigger is better, right? Bigger business, bigger lives, a bigger house! We thought, on some subconscious level, more space would equal a nicer life. We were coming apart at the seams in our little house, clutter everywhere, and we had another baby (the third child!) on the way. We were so excited we would finally have a place to put everything—and everyone.

The kids would each have their own bedrooms and so much space: We would finally have a home with separate kid space for toys and play, adult space for peace and quiet, and studio-office space for Mommy to write.

We briefly considered whether to buy an older home and renovate or buy new. We eventually decided everything new (and expensive) would work better and need less maintenance. We found the perfect home: new construction on almost an acre, two miles from the office and one mile from one of the best public elementary schools in the country.

I had some hesitation about going too big—this was a major leap—since I was the one who would have to manage it all, but we figured we would have enough money to hire help: a decorator, of course; nanny, chef, housekeeping; landscaping and maintenance. With enough paid professionals, bigger would definitely be better.

The Reality: *The bigger the house, the more work—and money—it takes to keep up.*

We ended up in our million-dollar Buckhead home on March 15, 2000—the very same day the stock market crashed and the technology bubble burst with an emphatic and irreversible bang. No one at the time realized how bad it would be. The company wouldn't be going public—in fact, we were in for a monumental struggle to keep the business going in a devastating economic downturn.

We were in Big Trouble, with a huge house, huge mortgage, far less cash than we had anticipated (all sunk into the house), rapidly dwindling "wealth," and increasing debt.

Aside from the financial burden and challenges we faced, we quickly learned the cold, hard realities of bigger and better. We now had 10,000 square feet: five bedrooms, five bathrooms, two half-baths (one "formal," one "informal," which was nicer than our family bathroom in the old house), a full basement, three-car garage, and a big landscaped yard, front and back.

The kids each had their own bedrooms and bathrooms—big mistake. They hated being alone and on the second floor, away from Mom and Dad. Children having their own bathrooms is also unwise—in our case, it was three times the mess, with the added danger of flooding sinks, toilets, and bath-tubs—and they would all rather use Mom and Dad's bathroom anyway. Our big garden tub-Jacuzzi became the family bath, complete with everyone's bubble bath, shampoos, and oh-so-elegant big basket of bathtub toys.

The whole idea of separate kid space and adult space is laughable now—no matter how much space you have, the kids want to be underfoot all the time; which is a good thing, because if you can't see them, they are probably off causing trouble, flooding bathrooms and what not. We now have toy baskets and kid cupboards in every room, including the office, to keep them busy, happy, and out of our stuff!

And then there's the whole issue of clutter: The more space you have, the more clutter procreates like bunnies. The first problem: You can never find what you're looking for because you have junk and hiding places all over the house. Instead of one table or cabinet or countertop dedicated to the accumulation and periodic dispersal of clutter, you end up with entire rooms lost to it: the garage, basement, attic, laundry room, "butler's pantry," even a special built-in desk, just for clutter, in the kitchen.

And when you do give in to organizing one area—usually in the desperate search to find something gone missing—all the other areas get even worse! You can never catch up.

As for the hired help I was so optimistic about—we couldn't afford it when we were struggling to keep up with the mortgage payments and property taxes. Even when I could afford it, I couldn't stand having someone around all the time and having to be responsible for more lives than the five I was already managing.

We thought we would be okay, as far as maintenance worries, since everything was brand-new. Wrong. Things just broke on a much larger scale: four air conditioners, instead of one; seven toilets instead of two; really expensive appliance repairs instead of easy replacement with a quick call to Sears. With such a big showplace of a house, prices went up as people came down the driveway. Nothing was small scale, or cheap.

We had enjoyed being outside in our old neighborhood, and spent a lot of time with our neighbors. The kids ran and played through the yards, which were all connected, and we used to sit out on the front porches, or in the front yards, and hang out together, waiting for all the working spouses to come down the street after work each night. In the bigger, better neighborhood, the houses are farther apart, the driveways are longer, and the yards are more cut off, with fences and landscaping. People come and go in the privacy of their multivehicle garages. Besides, we spend so much time inside, chasing clutter and keeping up with day-to-day life in a big house, there's no time to be outside, just hanging out. There's always too much to do.

The Rule: *Less is more, in houses as with many (but not all!) things in life.*

It truly isn't the size of the package, it's what you do with it that counts!

Rebel Rx:

1. Five hundred square feet per person is more than sufficient—more than many of us grew up with.

2. Children don't need or want their own "space"—it's just more to clean.

3. If all your junk mail and clutter doesn't fit in a laundry basket that you can hide away in a minute, you've got too much.

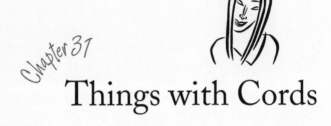

Things with Cords

Chapter 31

The Myth: *Men are born and raised with that special handyman ability.*

As a teenager, I daydreamed about the man I would marry. He would love, honor, and cherish me and, of course, fix things, too! I didn't want my mother's frustration, having married a man who was worthless with a hammer. (Sorry, Dad—it's true!) I would find a husband who could plow through the "honey-do list" in half an hour; rebuild my '65 Mustang—and keep it running; assemble anything that came into the house, with or without directions. No job would be too big.

His father would have taught my man all the basics of home repair, maintenance, and upgrades, from changing light bulbs and furnace filters to building a deck and putting in a sprinkler system. Together we would tackle Home Depot, take classes, and renovate the house of our dreams.

His golden hands were made for building and assembling. His agile mind would be a whiz at electronics, too. No stereo,

VCR, or computer would be too complicated for my technical hunk. Terminology like www, html, RAM, modem, VHS, DVD, surround sound, subwoofers . . . all would be part of his vocabulary. No problem.

The Reality: *Some men are hopeless when it comes to repairs.*

"Vic-ki! I can't get this thing to work!" It makes me think of Ozzy Osbourne yelling "Shar-on!" every time he can't figure out how to turn on the TV.

"The toilet is overflowing. . . . What do I do?!"

I made a "honey-do" list once. He laughed and said, "Who's that for?"

He promptly got rid of my '65 Mustang the first time it left us stranded on the highway, and bought me a Honda Accord with a three-year warranty and roadside assistance. Phrases like these are standard at our house:

"Call the builder, the oven light needs changing."

"Who's going to put *that* together?" (on Christmas Eve)

"Do you want to mow the lawn?"

"Honey, help! How does the computer turn on?"

"Can you fix this outlet so I can dry my hair?"

His father might have tried to teach him the basics of owning a home, but it went in one ear and out the other. I adjusted. I learned to be Fix-it Vik. When I need help, I turn to a handyman, my new best friend. He doesn't whine when I give him a list as long as his arm to fix. He doesn't say, "Can't you do any of this?"

The Golden Rule at my house is, If it comes with directions

or batteries, it's mine to deal with, including any and all toys. My husband came up with that one, of course. I toil over instructions without a single word in English. What's up with directions that have no words and pictures so small I need to get out the magnifying glass to see them? The problem is, once I locate the picture, I have no idea what it's supposed to be!

The biggest nightmare for me is the stuff that needs programming. Stereos, VCRs, and computers fall into this category. Learning to separate input, output, and audio has been helpful, but getting to know my handy, hunky, single neighbor was my insurance we would have music and TV in surround sound in this century. A little whine (not wine, although that might help, too), a sad look, and a bra-less tank top have hooked him into service on numerous occasions.

I know I am not alone. Many women out there are dealing with the challenges of home repair and technology. Our well-educated, career-driven men are somehow able to keep up with the most complex financial transactions and engineer modern miracles, but they are worthless when it comes to things with cords. They have not evolved. They still refuse to ask for directions. Unfortunately, once you've learned to do it yourself, there is no turning back: They know we can do it, so why should they even try?

The Rule: *Power is being able to do it yourself.*

Life is much easier when you learn to fix things yourself, or know who to call, instead of depending on your man to get things done. He will like your take-charge attitude and appreciate the "handywoman" in you.

Rebel Rx:

1. When in doubt: Power Off, Power On. If that or a good, swift kick doesn't fix it, call in a professional.
2. Keep your handyman's number on speed dial.
3. Have your own toolbox and hoard batteries—maybe your husband will get jealous and develop an interest.
4. Date Night: Take classes at Home Depot; it's fun.

Chapter 32

Housewife Fantasy

The Myth: *Real repairmen look just like the hunk on TV, so celebrate that broken dishwasher!*

Remember the Diet Coke Guy? His name was Lucky Vanous, and he was *hot*. In the 1990s, Lucky, as the half-naked construction worker provocatively swigging a Diet Coke in a sweaty moment, observed by a gaggle of ogling women from their office window, caused a huge sensation. For twenty- and thirtysomething working girls who would become the stay-at-home moms and housewives of today, that one commercial was the start: The Myth of the Hunky Handyman.

There's just something about a guy that works with his hands, especially when he looks that good. If that's what I have to look forward to as daytime entertainment, I just might be able to handle the at-home gig! I could see myself, home all day, calling upon these studly guys who would come at a moment's notice to fix whatever was broken. . . . Prince Valiant in a white pick-up truck with a tool belt. Bring it on!

The Reality: *TV commercials are not real life!*

Oh Honey, the sad reality of your typical repairman:

- Hunky is more likely chunky. Instead of an enticing view of a well-built chest and powerful arms . . . you get the rear view—a whole lot wider and further below the belt than you'd ever want to see.

- A moment's notice is more like "When I get around to it . . . next week or so," combined with the insipid anti-housewife attitude and assumption of "You ain't got nothing better to do than wait around on me, Little Lady."

- And then there is the whole "repair" misnomer in the title of repairman. . . . If you want it done right, you either do it yourself, nag your husband into doing it (and wait an extra month or so), or call on your father-in-law—by far the best option, because he will do it right the first time, usually by the end of the day, and he won't expect sex or money!

If you are waiting around for the Mythical Hunky Handyman, get ready to wait a long, long time. Better yet, turn on the TV—you are far more likely to catch an old rerun of the Diet Coke commercial.

However, every once in a while—and you never know when—you'll be at home expecting crusty old Bubba to come by and fix some switches or unplug a toilet . . . when he gets around to it, of course . . . you wouldn't have showered or dressed up because . . . well, why bother? Lo and behold, who shows up at your door? Bubba's younger brother/cousin/ trainee/whoever: Mike—a handsome stud worthy of Lucky's role in the commercial! What do you do? "Go ahead and get started. . . . Do you need anything? Coffee? Soda? (Me?) I'll check on you in a few minutes. . . . I think there is some other stuff broken too. . . . "

Grab the phone, run to your bathroom for the Instant Tornado (personal version): change clothes, wash your face, brush your hair, put on a little makeup, for God's sake! All at the same time, I speed dial Vicki: "Get over here—*now!* The electrician is here—you won't believe this one! No, I'm not calling for emergency back-up, really—you have to come over and see for yourself! Scrub up a bit—and pull out a few of your fuses or break a couple of light bulbs so you'll need him over at your house too!"

I know it's pitiful, but the opportunities to flirt with a captive audience in your own home are few and very far between— you've got to move fast!

The Rule: *Honor the Hot Handyman Referral Network.*

Rebel Housewives *must* stick together on this one: If you find one, you are required to pass him along! But before word gets out, be sure to have him do everything you can think of in your house (I'm talking about repairs and maintenance, Girls!)—chances are it will be a very long while before he gets back to you.

Rebel Rx:

1. Be prepared. The time you don't shower or get dressed is the time the Hunky Handyman will show up.

2. If they have vicious body odor, bad breath, or tobacco-stained teeth, don't stop to chat. Be busy. Hold the phone to your ear, whether there is someone on the other end or not.

3. Have a phone buddy back-up plan, in case of emergency—or in case your repairman is too chatty.

4. Sweet talkin' works every time, in any situation, and don't you forget it.

Chapter 33

A Whole Lotta Money, Honey

The Myth: *It's just as easy to fall in love with a rich man.*

Money does not grow on trees, as my dad used to say. As a young girl, I didn't think about money. I didn't grow up in a lavish lifestyle, but I grew up with all I needed, so I never had to give much thought to the matter. I just assumed I'd marry a guy who made loads of cash (or better yet, with a daddy who just handed it down); and, of course, being a product of the '80s, I would be *Superwoman*! I would run a company (what company, I didn't know), and by the time I was twenty-eight, make as much or more money than my successful husband, who would be CEO of a competing company (then we could trade secrets under the sheets!).

Our creed: We will live within our means. We will live off of one income and save the other. We will build our bank account so we will always have reserves. We will pay cash for everything, no debt for us. We will be rich, rich, rich! We will invest in the stock market and with all our knowledge, we'll buy low and sell high. Old Aunt Jane will remember us in her will, and our nest egg will be forever secure.

The Reality: *Trust fund babies don't grow on trees and love doesn't pay the mortgage.*

I haven't taken an official poll, but I think it's safe to say that 99 percent of the men out there are not trust fund babies and have to work. My chance of finding a trust fund baby whom I loved and who loved me was nil and none. The man I fell in love with in college (and later married) never minded letting me pay for dinner—he was always broke!

My naiveté was extraordinary. With a college degree under my arm, I was ready to do battle with anything and anyone. I figured it would take me a week or two to find a job and begin my corporate climb. (I knew I couldn't start out as president.) I was looking for those great fringe benefits: a private airplane, my own boardroom, and a hidden liquor cabinet in my private office.

What I got was a job making $16,700 doing the same thing I did while I was in college—selling clothes. I wasn't supposed to be peddling clothes; I was supposed to be bossing around thousands of people—you know, running things.

I wish money did grow on trees; it would *really* come in handy. Everything costs more than you ever would have expected. Let's start with the house: Stretching to buy the bigger house sounds good until you have to fill it up with furniture by opening credit cards that promise no payments for five years. Five years later, you realize you still don't have the money because now you have kids! Attached to the new house is a new garage that needs a new gas-guzzling SUV and of course—another payment.

It never occurred to me that preschool would cost more than my entire college education. How does one plan for that?

And what about those little surprise bills? The plumber who is supposed to unclog the toilet for $75 and then tells you it will be $875 because he has to take the toilet off the wall to rescue the half-dozen toys that have been flushed bye-bye?

We never saved any money on two incomes. How did we think we were going make it on one—with children? I don't think that transferring credit card balances from one card to another is considered a method of saving.

Maybe the secret is you never do catch up. Just when you think you have it all figured out—the money thing I mean—the stock market goes to pot and your 401(k) is worth nothing (should have spent it in our twenties) and you find out old Aunt Jane is penniless. It feels like you are back at ground zero, but now there is school to pay for, piano lessons, and an even bigger house to fill up with only one income, still borrowing money from mom and dad to make ends meet.

The only thing this Supermom ended up bossing around is two kids and a husband.

The Rule: *No matter what your income, you always need more.*

There are three ways to make the money stretch to the end of the month:

1. Cut spending. (You can never do that.)
2. Shorten the month. (I haven't figured out how to make everyone else go along with this one yet.)
3. Make more money, Honey! (This is the one we're working on.)

Rebel Rx:

1. Lesson of the '90s: Liquidate stock options as fast as they are vested.
2. Enjoy the DINK (Dual Income No Kids) lifestyle while you can; you'll probably never have as much money and freedom when you have kids.
3. Something's gotta give—downsize! You really don't need all that stuff.
4. Check old Aunt Jane's bank account before you spend your inheritance.
5. Keep buying those Lotto tickets!

PART SIX

How She Does It

Chapter 34

Kahlua in My Coffee

The Myth: *Perfection paves the road to domestic bliss.*

I have a friend—actually she's not really a friend, more of an acquaintance. Anyway, this woman is the modern-day June Cleaver: always put together, always beautiful, friendly, generous, calm. The updated incarnation of the Perfect Woman, she works full time, volunteers at school and in the community, keeps a spotless home (she found and can afford to keep the perfect housekeeper-nanny), and probably makes wild, passionate love to her very successful, perfect husband every night.

She is never exhausted, never has a headache, PMS, or a yeast infection. She is a vision of perfection: how the heck does she do it?

The Reality: *Nobody's life is perfect.*

Drugs, alcohol, and anti-depressants, that's my guess.

Although my world sometimes seems overpopulated with these perfect, happy, have-it-all, do-it-all, be-it-all women, the reality—my reality as a Rebel Housewife—is very different.

If I'm the example, I'll be honest: I never feel "put together"—who has the time? I'm a wash-and-wear girl, whatever is most comfortable, whatever is clean. I've had to greatly simplify my standards of beautiful: It no longer includes a full face of makeup and every hair in place. If I can get my teeth cleaned, face washed, and hair brushed and pulled back—and make sure three children and my husband have all done the same, with something in hand for breakfast before we race out the door to avoid another Tardy at school—that's a good day.

Friendly, generous, calm . . . I try, I really do, but I seem to operate on stress, always running from one place to be on time (give or take a few minutes) at the next. I prefer to use the carpool lane at preschool so I don't have to chitchat or see and be seen, particularly if I couldn't find anything clean, and I opted for comfort and starting a load of laundry on the way out, or a few precious minutes of sleep-in instead of ironing a fresh outfit.

I work full time and more, although I work at home and benefit from the flexibility and freedom of not having a boss or coworkers—or a regular paycheck. I volunteer at school once a week, and I'm only able to do that because I make it a priority over everything else—and because I can use it as an excuse to avoid any other volunteer opportunities. I do not have a spotless home—one week I decided to keep up with the laundry as my big goal, and the dishes didn't get done for seven days. I envy those women who can prepare a delicious, wholesome meal for their family every night *and* get the kitchen all cleaned up by bedtime. I could never find, much less afford, the perfect housekeeper-nanny, although I do have once-a-week cleaning help. She doesn't do kids, dishes, or laundry.

I make wild, passionate love to my husband . . . when we're off on a romantic weekend or the kids aren't home. Other than that, it's somewhat less wild, as passionate as possible, generally "quickie" love . . . when we're not exhausted by the time we both get to bed, and when I don't have a headache, PMS, or a yeast infection.

Since having my third child and moving to the perfection of Buckhead (an affluent Atlanta neighborhood), I take two prescription drugs every day: the first to prevent the arrival of any more children; the second to help me survive day to day with the ones I already have. And I put Kahlua in my coffee— hey, you do what you have to do to get by.

Perfection is a myth. We all get through the best we can. We're all entitled to have a bad day; sometimes it lasts a week, a month, or even a year. Remember Shirley Maclaine's line from *Steel Magnolias:* "I'm not crazy, M'Lynn. I've just been in a very bad mood for forty years!"

The Rule: *Keep it all in perspective.*

Be realistic and face each day with humor. Do the best you can and try not to worry about everybody else's expectations and opinions. If you have a bad day that lasts more than a week or two or a month—get help.

Rebel Rx:

1. Kahlua and rum both come in little single-serving sized bottles. If you are stuck all summer watching G-rated matinees in theaters full of screaming kids, at least have a little rum in your bucket of Coke (but just one)!

2. Organize and conquer: keep kids shoes and socks on a shoe rack and baskets in the garage or in a closet or hallway by the door. It will save you hours of trying to find matching socks and lost shoes in the heat of trying to get out the door.

3. Get walking. Regular outdoor exercise can save your sanity.

Chapter 35

Little White Lies

The Myth: *Honesty is the best policy in marriage, family, and life.*

The truth, and nothing but—right?

"How many men have I slept with? Well . . . forty, and the Italian Stallion could do *it* four times in one night! But that's all in the past, you Big Stud—you're the only one for me!" He won't mind, as long as I am honest and open with him.

"Truth be told, Honey, your mother is a really terrible cook!" I'm sure he already knows that, anyway.

"You can be honest with me. . . . Does this outfit make me look fat?"

"*Yes,* it is new! I spent $250 at the mall today!"

"Do you like what I've done with my hair?"

I'll let him know when he needs a new haircut, if his belly is getting big, when he's acting like his father (and should knock it off)—straightforward, good, old-fashioned honesty. That's what it's all about.

And honesty with the children—that is really important. How can they grow up to be good citizens and trustworthy adults if we don't tell them the truth? Santa Claus? The Easter Bunny? The Tooth Fairy? Is it really such a good idea to raise children believing in omnipotent old guys who "always *know*" and can break and enter our home at will, squeezing down the chimney no less, to dispense rewards and retribution based on behavior? The mythical rabbit that actually wants all those messy colored eggs and brings baskets-full of candy—whose idea was this? And the Tooth Fairy . . . wouldn't it be better to pay kids to brush their teeth, rather than encouraging them to hope for their teeth to fall out for a little monetary compensation? With proper parenting and absolute honesty, our children wouldn't need all the lies and fantasy, and we'd all be better off!

The Reality: *We all need "little white lies" to get by—to make life a little more pleasant, to make things a whole lot easier on everybody.*

"I said *four*, Honey, not forty—and not one of them was as good as you!"

"I love your mother's turkey casserole. It's so, so turkey-like!" (Thinking, "This tastes like an old rubber shoe and I can't believe he loves it.")

"But it's hamburger."

"Oh yeah, I knew that—yum!"

The truth is there are most definitely things I do *not* want to know. I'd better look "Fantastic!" in whatever I put on. I don't need him to tell me it looks as if I've gained a few pounds—I'm well aware of that, because my jeans don't fit. I want him to lie to me and tell me I look the same—just as beautiful, maybe even more—as the day we were married.

I prefer the policy of "Don't ask, don't tell" whenever I spend an afternoon at the mall, and I will always resort to the fallback of "This old thing? It's been in the closet for ages!" It keeps both of us much happier. And let's be clear: There is *never* a reason for him to say he doesn't like my hair, whether I'm blonde, a redhead, spiked, whacked, or frizzed. The only words I need to hear are, "You look ten years younger!"

Imagine straight-up honesty with your husband regarding the length (or lack of) his hair (or anything else); the "love handles" he's growing out just for you; or, heaven forbid, his choice of clothing . . . that's just plain cruel! And, believe me, there will be no sparkly baubles or wonderful surprises on your anniversary if you tell him he's starting to sound just like his father . . . even if it's true!

It's imperative with children—how else would you get from January 1 through December 25 without the threat of Santa Claus bringing a piece of coal instead of toys? The Easter Bunny is not only useful to legitimately bring all your favorite candy into the house, he serves as an important reminder throughout the year to be kind to animals. He is the Herald of Spring, the protector of small animals children might otherwise be tempted to torture—but not if the Easter Bunny is watching! I'm still not wild about the Tooth Fairy, but reminding the kids that the Tooth Fairy doesn't want to be collecting scungy teeth—she'll probably pay less—seems to help motivate them to brush.

We use the factitious "Kid Police" all the time, particularly at bedtime. These very strict policemen roam neighborhoods to make sure all children are in bed at a proper time. If not, they take the kids and parents to jail (where there are no toys!). For extra effect, my husband sometimes rings the doorbell and shines a flashlight in the window. Hey, it works!

The Rule: *Learn to keep your mouth shut so your foot can't get in!*

There are some truths better left untold. It's better to tell a little white lie than to be outright mean—to anyone.

Rebel Rx:

1. Zip it! Zip it quick!
2. If you can't say something nice . . . make something up.
3. Be kind: When he gains ten pounds and can't get his jeans zipped up, tell him they must have shrunk in the wash.
4. *Warning:* Never say anything in front of kids that you don't want repeated—they'll call you out in a little white lie every time!

Chapter 36

Mom Knows All

The Myth: *Mother knows everything.*

She's supposed to, anyway. My mother certainly did. She always knew—everything:

When I hadn't done something I said I did: "Yes, I cleaned my room."

When I did do something I said I hadn't: "No, I didn't borrow your pink and purple sparkly earrings."

When I tried to slack off, short cut, or take the easy way out: "It's clean!"

She knew.

She knew I cleaned my room by shoving everything under the bed. She didn't even have to go upstairs to check.

"Go find my earrings in that mess you just pushed under your bed—and don't roll your eyes at me, Young Lady."

It was like the woman had eyes on the back of her head. They were functional, all knowing, and extremely accurate—

until I was about fifteen, when I finally figured out that my mother's omnipotence was showing signs of aging. But until then—she had it, and I was stone-cold busted, every time.

The Reality: *Mothers intuition is lucky guesswork.*

I still haven't found the extra set of eyes I'm supposed to have in the back of my head. With my oldest child already nine years old, I'm running out of time! I've had to improvise:

"Zach, brush your teeth."

"I did already!"

"No, you didn't. Go brush your teeth." (I was taking a chance, listening to some little whisper of intuition.)

The first time it worked—he went back to the bathroom and brushed his teeth!

The next day:

"Zach, brush your teeth."

"I did already!"

"No, you didn't. Go brush your teeth."

"Mooommmm, I *did!*" (Somewhat convincing, but still . . .)

"Okay, I'm going to check your toothbrush—if it is still dry—"

It worked again! He was off running to brush his teeth before I could check.

The third day:

"Zach, brush your teeth."

"I did already!"

"Are you sure?"

"My toothbrush is wet and everything!"

"Zach, go brush your teeth."

"Awwwww. How do you always know?"

Now that I'm a more experienced mom, I know full well mothers can't keep up with everything. I still can't find the extra eyes, but there is some powerful maternal intuition available, if we listen. Intuition based on experience, educated guesswork, and observation—and when all that fails, as long as you *act* like you know everything . . . well, then, maybe you can get by for fifteen or sixteen years.

The Rule: *Listen—and use your intuition.*

Take wild guesses and be confident—you will really impress your kids with your second sight!

Rebel Rx:

1. If they won't look you in the eye, something is going on.
2. Body language is very telling, especially in kids.
3. Train Daddy to always answer, "Whatever Mommy said . . . "
4. Always keep them guessing—never answer "How did you know?" especially if you just got lucky!

Chapter 37

Mommy Dearest

The Myth: *Other mothers don't ever break down.*

The child throws herself on the grocery store floor littered with produce droppings and goes into a fit that resembles an epileptic seizure. The mother gently picks her up, strokes her hair, and sweetly whispers words into her ear that have a soothing, calming effect on the little girl.

The mother must have nerves of steel. It's amazing how some women really can have it all—the career, the children, the wardrobe! She's so put together: makeup perfect, nails manicured, hair all in place. I bet her house is clean, her car is washed, and her laundry is ironed and folded, too.

Some moms don't seem to have a breaking point. They can take anything. There is no deep furrow between her brows from worrying about her children's academic success, or whether her children are going to use their manners and mind their p's and q's. I bet her children make their beds every day and always pick up their toys, and when they don't—well, it's no big deal. She takes it all with a grain of salt. It doesn't matter that she spent all night doing the laundry (after she worked all day) and her daughter played dress-up while pretending to be a pig rolling in the mud. She smiles gracefully and reminds her daughter of how hard Mommy works and please don't play dress-up in her school clothes.

The Reality: *We all have breaking points.*

Know that behind every mother is a breakdown; most of us are just smart enough to do it off camera. Some moms might take a little longer, but eventually we all get there. I can imagine the words the mom in the grocery store was really whispering to her child:

"Get up off the floor now or when we get home you will spend the rest of your life in your room!"

I start my day with the Tornado, picking up everything in my path, including the spilled glass of milk Lillian manages to leave for me every morning. I then scrape the toothpaste off the counter—why do they always leave dried toothpaste everywhere?—and clean the dog doo doo off my son's tennis shoes. I'm still calm.

I spend the next hour packing the swim stuff so I can take the kids swimming. We arrive, get our suits on, settle in, and I open a magazine I have been trying to read for three months. Ten minutes later, the kids whine, "The water is too cold!" They want to go home. I endure the whining for an additional ten minutes, but finally give up and we pack up and return home. I'm still calm.

"Mom, I'm bored. I have no one to play with."

"We were just at the pool with fifty other kids, don't you remember? And you wanted to go home!"

"Can we go back?"

"No." I am still calm.

As we are debating the swimming pool, I look down and discover I am standing in a puddle of water in my living room. My daughter has plugged up the toilet again and it's been overflowing since we left. The water has made its way through the ceiling and is pouring down through the light fixture. I grab the plunger, a bucket, and a mop and begin my plumber duties. I am still calm.

After I get the floor cleaned up, the dog vomits at my feet some kind of critter that she has eaten for lunch. I am still calm.

The phone rings and it's my husband, asking if I would mind running to the post office to overnight the taxes so they aren't late. Fine. I haul both tired kids in the car and go. Lillian complains she's not feeling well. I carry her inside. In line at the post office, my son takes all the envelopes and throws them all over the floor. I calmly tell him to pick them up; he sticks out his tongue. I smile at the other people in line.

"He's tired, excuse him."

I pick up the envelopes while holding Lillian. I get the package mailed, get back in the car, and it won't start. I call roadside assistance and wait for an hour for them to show up and tell me I'm out of gas. Didn't Brad fill it this weekend? Apparently not. I manage to get some gas and make it home. I'm still calm.

My husband gets home from work.

"Did you pick up my shirts at the dry cleaner?"

"No!" I scream, finally reaching the breaking point where I turn into Mommy Dearest and start screaming something about wire hangers.

"Kids, go to your room and don't come out—ever! Brad, slavery went out over 100 years ago, do your own goddamn errands! I'm done. I give up. I'm through."

I am not calm.

The Rule: *It's okay to snap.*

Run to your bedroom, close the door, and let out a primal scream—it feels really good! Get it out of your system. Reset. Start over.

Rebel Rx:

1. Walk. It's amazing how walking can clear your head.
2. A little shot of tequila does wonders.
3. Make sure to have a phone friend; unload the day's woes.
4. Have sex—some good sex takes the day's stress off.
5. Go back to Chapter 34, "Kahlua in My Coffee" for help.

Chapter 38

Mom's Getaway

The Myth: *I'll always love being called Mom.*

The first time my son called me "Mommy," I cried. Actually, he called me "Ma-Ma," and it sounded like "Ba-Ba," but let's not get technical—I knew what he was saying. I was suddenly transformed from "Vicki" to "Mommy," and my life would never be the same. The former individual Vicki was now a mom, with all the responsibility that word, in all its various manifestations, entails.

"Moooooommy! Where are my socks?" Apparently, no one but Mom knows where socks are kept.

"Mom, I need a Band-Aid!" Only moms have healing power.

"You are the meanest mom in the world!" Which is what Clayton says when he is sent to his room.

"You're the best mom in the world!" Which is what Lillian says when I give her ice cream before dinner.

As my kids got older, the use of the word *mom* expanded as their friends addressed me:

"Hello, Clayton's mom."

"Lillian's mom, can I have a snack?"

One time I counted how many times the word *mom* was said in our house—103 times in one day. Even Brad was calling me Mom. Vicki just seemed to disappear, and this new creature took charge.

I thought I was ready for the transformation—I was ready for mom-hood. I was ready to say goodbye to Vicki and embrace the new me—Mom, Mommy, Mother . . . yep, that's me!

The Reality: *What's my real name?*

I can vividly recall every time I have been away by myself since both kids were born: exactly two times. I don't mean away with my husband; I mean all by myself, when I got to be just Vicki for at least two consecutive days with an overnight. Two glorious times.

The first escape was a trip to London to surprise my auntie for her seventieth birthday. Before I left Brad and the kids, I worked for weeks making lists of what to do and where everything was located, including the socks. I premade meals and stocked the refrigerator and the pantry. I arranged play dates for the kids and begged favors from all my friends to help out. At one point, I wondered if it was even worth going. All the work just to get everybody ready for me to leave left me exhausted, but I kept thinking about five whole days to be Vicki.

During those five days in London, I woke up when I wanted, ate when I wanted, went to the bathroom all by myself—uninterrupted—and went anywhere I wanted. It was complete freedom. I even went to a pub with my sister—and men I didn't know chatted with me! No one had any idea of my alter ego. Mom was resting and Vicki was out!

The second time Vicki got to surface went a little differently. Vicki had been suppressed for a long time, and when she saw the opportunity to get out, she grabbed it.

"Brad, my Aunt Sally passed away and I have to go the funeral. You'll need to take off work and look after the kids. I'm leaving in an hour."

"An hour? What's the rush?"

"It's the only flight." (Lie.)

No careful preparation this time. There wasn't a morsel of food in the house, but I didn't care. I knew Brad wouldn't let them starve. I arrived at the airport two hours early with one small carry-on. No schlepping, no one telling me they're hungry, no one spilling on me, no one telling me not to buy three magazines for my flight because they cost twice as much at the airport—just beautiful peace and quiet. I could hear myself think. I found my way to Starbucks, ordered a latte, and sat down to people-watch. I observed the typical chaos that all moms endure when traveling with children: the whining, the fighting, and let's not forget the schlepping. I enjoyed every minute of my latte and then boarded the plane.

I arrived in Minneapolis and my mother and auntie (not the one who died, the one I spent the seventieth birthday with) picked me up at the airport. I knew they were excited to see me; I can't remember the last time they met me at the airport. The minute I saw them, we all started talking at once, chatting about my quick exit and leaving Brad with the kids. Auntie commented on how happy I was. I told her, "I feel so free!" Like a tiger who had been let out of its cage for a day.

We arrived at my childhood home, and I realized I hadn't been home by myself in more than seven years! No one to entertain, no one to cook for, no one get up for, no one to mother! My mom was taking care of me! We broke open the champagne to celebrate the fact I was home, home alone. I had my parents all to myself. My dad and I stayed up until midnight toasting to life, and we finished off the night with a cigar. I slept in until nine o'clock, and my mom made me breakfast. My dad took off from his usual hunting to spend the day with me. We went out to lunch and bummed around. I almost forgot I was there for a funeral, I was having so much fun doing nothing! My mom asked me if I was going to call home. I said, "No," reassuring her that Brad could handle it.

The next day was the funeral, and I gathered with all my family, most of whom I hadn't seen in twenty years. We hugged, laughed, and reminisced about our childhoods. Again that night my mother made dinner and waited on me hand and foot. She even did my laundry so I wouldn't have to wash anything when I got home. As I got ready to leave and go home I said a prayer to my recently deceased aunt:

"Thank you, Aunt Sally, for giving me the greatest gift: The gift of coming home and getting to be 'just Vicki' again."

I boarded the plane and smiled to myself—who knew returning home for a funeral would be my greatest holiday of all? I felt revived and ready to return home. I walked in the door to my house and the first words I heard were, *"Mommy we missed you!"* Vicki happily settled in to be Mom again—until next time.

The Rule: *Take time to escape by yourself once in a while.*

Once a mom always a mom, but you need time to yourself, too.

Rebel Rx:

1. Enjoy carrying a small purse on your Mom's Getaway—you don't have to haul anyone else's stuff!

2. It doesn't take a fancy trip. A getaway can be anything: a conference, a day at the spa, or even a funeral.

3. Get involved in something not related to being a parent, something that is just for you.

4. Let your hubby be with the kids by himself for a few days and "wing it"—he'll give you the royal treatment when you get home!

Keeping it All in Perspective

At the bottom of it all, at the end of the day, we think we can make life perfect for everyone. That's our job, isn't it? We promised to love and honor (I had *obey* taken out of my wedding vows—just couldn't do it!) . . . and then when the kids came along, we committed to nurture them, protect them, educate them, and make sure they carried forward beautiful memories of a perfect, happy childhood with a perfect mother, always loving, kind, patient, and wonderful. That's a tall order, even for Superwoman.

God forbid we have a bad day—they could be scarred for life! One moment of impatience, one episode of lost temper, justified or not, one bad day, and I'm sorry—you have a drug addict or a school shooter on your hands. Not.

At the end of the day, even if it's been a really, really bad day—everybody was sick, the kids were home all day, Daddy was out of town on business, everything went wrong, and

Mommy Dearest made an appearance—get a little perspective by asking your kids, just before you turn the lights out and say good night for the last time, "How was your day today?"

Invariably, no matter how bad it was, your kids will give you those beautiful smiles and snuggly hugs and answer, "I had a *great* day, Mommy—I love you!"

Keep it all in perspective. All you can do is all you can do—live, love, laugh. Do the best you can—hubby still loves you, your kids still love you. Look forward to tomorrow's adventure—one day at a time, Baby.

Are You a Rebel Housewife?

We would love to hear from you!

Visit *www.RebelHousewife.com*. Subscribe to The Rebel Housewife Weekly Update online for Weekly Features:

The Rebel Housewife Column

Rebel Cooks! Recipes

Rebel Reviews! Books, Movies, Products, News

Specials: Contests, Promotions, vents

The Rebel Housewife is Time Out for Moms!

Our mission is to entertain, inform, commiserate, and provide a much-needed outlet and diversion for Rebel Housewives everywhere with The Rebel Housewife books, Web site, newsletter, and other resources: grown-up interaction, community, support, entertainment, and lots of laughter.

We hope you'll join the conversation and enjoy the ride. We can guarantee it will be fun—how could it *not* be, when you get involved with a rowdy pack of Rebel Housewives?

About the Authors

The Rebel Housewives are Sherri Caldwell (The Redhead) and Vicki Todd (The Blonde): wives, mothers, writers, best friends, and former neighbors in Atlanta, Georgia.

Sherri lives with her husband, Russ, their three children and two dogs in Atlanta.

Vicki, with her husband, Brad, their two children, Lucy the Great Dane, and Beauregard the Bunny relocated to Hong Kong in early 2004.

To Our Readers

Conari Press, an imprint of Red Wheel/Weiser, publishes books on topics ranging from spirituality, personal growth, and relationships to women's issues, parenting, and social issues. Our mission is to publish quality books that will make a difference in people's lives—how we feel about ourselves and how we relate to one another. We value integrity, compassion, and receptivity, both in the books we publish and in the way we do business.

Our readers are our most important resource, and we value your input, suggestions, and ideas about what you would like to see published. Please feel free to contact us, to request our latest book catalog, or to be added to our mailing list.

Conari Press
An imprint of Red Wheel/Weiser, LLC
P.O. Box 612
York Beach, ME 03910-0612
www.conari.com